CONFRONTATIONS
WITH MYSELF

Books by Helene Deutsch, M.D.

Neuroses and Character Types

The Psychology of Women

Selected Problems of Adolescence

A Psychoanalytic Study of the Myth
of Dionysus and Apollo

Confrontations with Myself

Confrontations with Myself

AN EPILOGUE

Helene Deutsch, M.D.

W · W · Norton & Company · Inc · New York

Copyright © 1973 by W. W. Norton & Company, Inc.

First Edition

Library of Congress Cataloging in Publication Data

Deutsch, Helene, 1884–
  Confrontations with myself.

  Includes bibliographical references.
  1. Deutsch, Helene, 1884–   2. Psychiatrists—
Correspondence, reminiscences, etc.   I.   Title.
RC339.S2.D48A33   1973   616.8'9'00924 [B]   73-4380
ISBN 0-393-07472-2

designed by Paula Wiener

PRINTED IN THE UNITED STATES OF AMERICA

1 2 3 4 5 6 7 8 9 0

To the memory of my husband

CONTENTS

ILLUSTRATIONS

Between pages 94 and 95

1. Wilhelm Rosenbach
2. Regina Fass Rosenbach
3. Hala at age 5
4. Bookplate designed for Helene Deutsch by her husband
5. Gisela and her children: Irena, Arthur, and Leonard
6. Felix and Helene Deutsch at the time of their marriage in 1912
7. Freud in his study in Vienna with his dog Lün
8. Helene Deutsch in 1936
9. On the farm at Babayaga

PREFACE

ONLY AFTER completing this autobiography did I realize that it forms a supplement to the autobiography hidden in my general work *The Psychology of Women*.[1] That is why I have decided to call this book an epilogue. I feel that the phrase "one for all and all for one" could serve as a motto for my collected works, including this autobiography—a collection I would entitle simply *The Woman*.

I would like to express especial gratitude to my friend Dr. Gregory Rochlin—a faithful ally against the gaining enemy, old age, since it was at his suggestion that I began to write this book. Presently head of the Children's Department of the Massachusetts Mental Health Center, he is also a prolific writer. His two main works are *Griefs and Discontents: The Forces of Change*[2] and the recent *Man's Aggression*.[3]

The original version of my book was written partly in English and partly in German. Mrs. Gerta Prosser deserves my thanks for helping to prepare the final English version. I must also thank those friends who read the manuscript and supplied helpful criticism, especially Drs. Ruth and Kurt Eissler and Drs. Ingrid and Sanford Gifford. Finally, Miss Laimdota Mazzarins deserves special thanks for taking time from her academic work in order to collaborate intensively on my work in all its stages.

1. New York: Grune & Stratton, 1944; now available also as a Bantam Books paperback.
2. Boston: Little, Brown & Company, 1965.
3. Boston: Gambit, Inc., 1972.

INTRODUCTION

AN OLD PERSON'S memoirs are written under certain distinct psychobiological conditions that differ only slightly from one individual to another. It seems that the process of sublimation active in the writing of autobiography and the weakening of sexual impulses create an atmosphere for the free welling-up of memories. "The memories that emerge from oblivion are more beautiful than the experiences themselves," Proust said; and this positive element lends them a vitality that works against the process of forgetting.

Another reason for the release of memories is the waning of the punitive force of the superego. One is old, the limitations on one's existence grow greater, and the nearness of death must be accepted as one more biological cruelty. The inner mechanisms geared to the future must be given up, and this further clears the way for the return of the past.

We expect, with reason, that the long years of living will have given us some degree of objectivity toward ourselves. This should allow the past and present at last to be evaluated truly. On the other hand, far-reaching psychic distortions may come into play as the old person struggles to preserve his weakening sense of identity. An example of this is the well-known tendency toward paranoia in old age. And one can often observe how an aging person actively resists the deterioration of his faculties, trying to protect himself by pretending it isn't happening; above all, how he embellishes the past, in order to find at least some comfort in a glorious "I was." It is a great psychic achievement to accept the disillusioning present just as it is, yet at the same time preserve the values that still remain.

I myself have the feeling, now that the biological end of my existence is near, that I have reached a height from which to review my life's achievements and disappointments. I would like to relive them and set them down *sine ira et studio* in the form of a short autobiography. This is a challenge; and I hope I will succeed, while my identity is still intact, in re-creating the story of my life—what I was once and what I am now. I also hope that the poet who with his creative fantasy lies hidden within each one of us will not make a "literary" tale out of my personal reality.

Everyone lives two lives simultaneously. One of them is devoted to adapting to the outside world and improving one's external circumstances. The other consists of fantasies, longings, distortions of reality, undertakings unfinished, achievements not won. And sometimes, in certain individuals, a double personality takes shape, combining "this is what I really am" with "this is what I want and picture myself to be."

During this time of being alone and very lonely, I have felt an increasing necessity to bring back my past life, my past self, by setting it down in writing. Is my deep loneliness the origin of this need? "Loneliness" is a word everyone thinks he understands. I have come to my own precise definition: that person is lonely who has no one for whom he or she is Number One. And this condition has awakened in me a hunger to fill my depleted existence with the past. By the time this narrative is finished, I shall know whether I can recommend the writing of an autobiography to other lonely people whose lives are nearly at an end.

When a person who has devoted her life to the study and practice of psychoanalysis sets about writing an autobiography, the suspicion naturally arises that the work will be a self-analysis —either made *ad hoc* or derived from one made previously. I shall not discuss at length the difference between a self-analysis and the memoirs of a psychoanalyst, but merely bring up the

obvious fact that whereas free association is the essence of psychoanalysis, in autobiography it is by no means fundamental. Autobiography is a process that is under firmer self-control than the
analytic method of free association. For that reason I am amazed
at how often memories I recognize as long buried beyond the
reach of consciousness—yes, memories that have even eluded
thorough psychoanalysis—readily come back without any serious
resistance as I write my autobiography.

The immense enhancement of my life that comes from writing
these memoirs does not lie in "knowing myself" nor in any renewed possibility of correcting old errors, expiating wrongs committed, retracting poor judgments, etc. It lies in the memory
process itself: the intense emotions that arise when we meet or
confront once more the loved and hated figures of the past.

I have learned during this writing that even given the sincerest
effort to be objective, each memory is shaped more or less by one's
current psychic condition, as well as by this memory's continuing
influence on one's life as a whole. Sometimes a minute incident,
harmless in itself, acquires in one's memory a lasting significance.
For example: in the Polish town where I was born lived a pen-
sioned army surgeon who had set up a civilian practice after his
retirement. He was what is called a *feldscher* in the army—that
is, a doctor who had never been to medical school. He spoke
broken Polish and generally used German instead. He was called
in once when I was a little girl and suffered from a bad stomach
ache. He pressed my stomach here and there, and when I cried
out at an especially painful squeeze, he exclaimed, using a popular expression: "Aha! So that's where the dog's hiding!" For many
years the belief lived on in my unconscious that I had a dog in
my belly. Only now have I learned to see the humorous side of my
childish conviction. But I can still recognize it in very distinct
dreams and I am aware of its psychic meaning. The dog appeared
again in a dream I had after my son was born, that time as a
danger to the newborn child.

From such recollections I have, strange to say, sometimes
learned more about myself than from psychoanalysis; I have come

to the conclusion that memories loaded with guilt feelings offer less resistance if they are called up in the course of autobiography as an objective historical report on oneself. Memories having to do with active infantile masturbation and sexual excitement, for instance, seem to remain for years in amnesia. Only now can I clearly recall that throughout early childhood my small girl-friends and I had a passion for sliding down the banister in my house, often at the risk of severe injury. The particulars of this game were repressed because they were associated with other and forbidden practices of a directly erotic nature.

It is hard to determine how old I was then, though in some cases I can ascertain my age from surrounding details: for example, Minnie, one of my childhood playmates, disappeared from my life when her father was promoted to a higher rank in the army and sent to a more prestigious garrison. Minnie was two years older than I, and was just about to enter school when she moved away. So I must have been less than four years old during this first blooming of sexual play. In psychoanalysis, my childhood before age five remained fairly dim, and it seemed as though not much had happened in that period.

One final note: readers who identify me as one of Freud's personal pupils may expect this book to contain new material about Freud. They will be disappointed. My intention has not been to reinterpret or add to Freud's biography—for nothing is so difficult as writing the biography of a genius. I have largely restricted myself to a report of my personal contacts with him. Ernest Jones' three-volume biography of Freud [1] is extensive, and one would expect that during this and future generations more books devoted entirely to Freud will be written. It is frustrating to limit myself to material of a personal nature—but the fact is that I am writing autobiography, and must remain within the boundaries of its form.

1. Ernest Jones, *Freud* (New York: Basic Books, 1957).

CONFRONTATIONS
WITH MYSELF

I

Przemyśl

PRZEMYŚL, where I was born on October 9, 1884, is a middle-sized town in Galicia, the section of Poland which through historical fate became part of the Austro-Hungarian Empire in 1772. It is a pleasant town on the river San, at the foot of picturesque remains of a fortress surviving from the glorious time of the Sobieskis and their victories over the Turks. These ruins themselves have served in more recent wars,[1] so that the name of the town, though difficult to pronounce, is widely known.

I know many people from Przemyśl who would rather have been born somewhere else. I remember that when I went to Vienna to study medicine and was looking for a room to rent, landladies asked me where I came from, and when they heard the names "Przemyśl" and "Poland" their friendly smiles disappeared. Their next question was invariably: "What religion are the Poles in Przemyśl?" I knew what they meant and would answer, "Mostly Jewish."

I did not spend many years in Przemyśl in relation to the rest

1. Przemyśl was besieged twice by the Russians in 1914.

of my life, but it remains for me the center of the earth. To this day I recall every smallest corner of the *Schlossberg*, the park built over the ruins of the old fort on the hill, especially the little hidden benches, which are probably still there, providing the same refuge for lovers that they did in my time. And I remember the surrounding hills and slopes; I wandered there hour after hour. It was an easy walk from our house in the center of town; either of two roads would take me, past various churches, to the *Schlossberg* in less than half an hour.

I have traveled much since then, and experienced with rapture many of the world's wonders, but have never lost my true love for the beauty of my home town. Were the sunsets over the *Schlossberg* hill as fiery red as I remember them? Was the full moon over the San quite as strange and ghostly? And was the little girl's impatience—"If only *I* were big and *you* were little . . ."—any different from that of other children?

Proust wrote: "In reminiscence my experiences do not fade, they grow more vivid, more beautiful or more ugly, but above all, *more significant.*" Once aroused from their sleep, the spirits I have called up out of the hills of my native town can only be stilled again by a true confrontation.

That is why, before I turn to those events in my life which may be of more general interest and indicate what my destiny was to be and what other people were involved in it, I would like to follow my heart and describe not only the town but also the house where I was born and the others who lived in it then.

Some time ago I asked a colleague who was going to Przemyśl for professional reasons if he would find out for me whether the Gizowski place, where I lived until late adolescence, was still standing. I don't know what he found out, but I suspect that his silence on the subject was due to tact—he must have felt that such a run-down building could not be the home of respectable people. Yet a number of prominent members of the town lived there; for instance, my father was a widely known and respected lawyer.

The house was a microcosm of the Polish-Jewish society of Przemyśl at that time. It was also quite interesting architecturally. In its center was a large courtyard and the three floors went up around it, containing tenants of widely differing social status. When I was in Seville strolling from one house to another and delighting in their attractive inner courts, I contrasted them in my thoughts with the shabby courtyard of the Gizowski house, where we had to put up with so many discomforts in our daily lives.

Standing in the heart of the town, on the *Ringplatz,* the house was separated from the regular traffic by a tiny public garden. Our balcony, in the front, was a box seat where we could observe the flow of the town's life rushing by. Sitting there at twilight we could spy on the love life of maids and soldiers, high-school boys and girls, and sometimes the sinful carrying-on of respectable married men. We could also see from there which tenant was late coming home at night. Sometimes a straggler had to wait outside a long time before the old caretaker, aroused from deep sleep by the doorbell, would appear in his grimy underwear. His hand would already be stretched out for the tip he considered a mandatory fee for opening the gate. I can hear my own voice: "Mr. Horak, I haven't got any change, I'll pay you tomorrow." Did I ever pay Mr. Horak as I promised, or have I remained his debtor to this day?

Now and then I have a daydream in which Mr. Horak and his family have found their way to my house in America (they must all be dead by now, since tuberculosis was their only family legacy) and I give him back in American money all the *groschen* I owe him. He cannot understand why I am being so noble— Horak never had much experience of human nobility. But he and I were on good terms: many a night, while the whole house lay in sleep except for me, it so happened that my beloved would steal into the courtyard with Horak's help to look up just once at the window of the room where I was studying for an examina- tion. Horak had learned tolerance: he was a devout Catholic but had two daughters who were full-time prostitutes. I never knew Mrs. Horak when she wasn't pregnant, and there was always a squalling baby around, generally left in the care of its prostitute sisters. Rather frequently we saw tiny coffins passing through their door, and often a priest, congratulating himself that his pious teaching was bearing such goodly fruit.

I often saw that same priest on the streets, on his way to administer extreme unction to a dying soul. These encounters, so frequent that they should have become a matter of indifference to me, never failed to move me. The sight has lasted in my memory all my life: the priest in his white lace surplice holding before him the viaticum, followed by a hunch-backed altar boy carrying the censer and a shrill little bell, which he shook constantly to remind the faithful to kneel down. All the passersby would sink to their knees like wheatstalks in the wind. I alone, the Jew, would remain standing in solemn silence. I felt marked by a stigma and full of shame. I did not belong.

This repeated sight not only exacerbated my inner problem of Catholic vs. Jewish, it must also have affected my concept of death. I know that for many years of my childhood I supposed that dying was an attribute of Catholics almost exclusively; Jews only died if they were very poor, which was certainly not the case with my family, the Rosenbachs. My strange idea may have come from the fact that to my knowledge none of the Rosenbachs died during my childhood.

The Horaks were not the only tenants of the dilapidated so-called apartments on the ground floor. In another damp corner lived an old house painter with his two sons: a motherless household, not happy but, so to speak, functioning. One day, probably when I was a very small girl, I was standing in the courtyard watching the not very exciting activities going on around me. The painter had just got dressed for work when a tile fell from God knows where right on the head of one of his sons, with such force that the brain was exposed. My memory presents me with the brains lying neatly on a plate as if ready to be served. Thus our early recollections condense and merge with later ones, in the end to become what we ourselves have made them.

But to continue the tour around the courtyard: in a better part of the ground floor lived my beloved *Babcia* (grandmother) Rosenbach and her two daughters Frania and Sonja. Later in the story these members of my family will play important roles. The remaining first-floor tenant was a figure of mystery . . . Mrs. N., a lady always dressed in black, whose features were scarcely visible under a thick coating of white makeup. She was known in the neighborhood as "The Pale Countess." Her room was next to the toilets. A small cookstove made it the most overheated place in the building. We children were forbidden to enter it, which is probably why it fascinated us, most of all me. From Mrs. N.'s room I often heard my mother in the hall calling, "Hala! Hala!" but I wouldn't answer for fear of getting a beating if I stepped out the door.

Mrs. N. had no husband but had one small daughter named Stella, with thin gold-blonde hair and blue squinting eyes. The child's dresses were made from richly colored silks and velvets. The fantasies of the Pale Countess were obviously expressed in these clothes. Mrs. N. gave a *groschen* to every beggar who knocked on her door, along with these words: "Pray for the soul of Hugo von Willbrigenz." I suspect that this non-Polish name belonged to some officer who was the father of Stella.

The Pale Countess supported herself by telling fortunes from the cards and giving French lessons. Her clientele consisted mostly of servants, who credulously believed all her predictions. She used to put Stella to bed in the evening and disappear, to return later with bags of goodies for her darling. She seemed determined to create around Stella an aura of affluence. I would guess that she was one of those now almost legendary figures, a daughter banished from home for bearing an illegitimate child. She would have made a fascinating subject for a study of unwed mothers in the higher social classes of that era.

On the second floor lived the "aristocracy" of the house: my parents, my brother and two sisters and I; and another lawyer's family, the Tarnawskis. There was one son in this family: Tadzio, an introverted, lonely child whose mother, probably suffering from an anxiety neurosis, never let him out of her sight. Tadzio grew up to be a poet . . . but our paths separated. In my memory the Tarnawskis remain as the finest representatives of those rare Polish patriots who accepted readily the equal standing of Polish Jews.

(I have seen three generations of Jews suffer to a greater or lesser degree under Polish anti-Semitism. Nothing is as odious to me as the often-heard remark: "If only all Jews were like *you*. . . ." Nevertheless I am aware that the fate of the Jews developed in them qualities that made them unloved in the world. In Poland, they had everything against them: social conditions, their own religious fanaticism, the difficulty of breaking out of the walls of the ghetto, as well as the Polish people's deep-seated belief that the Jews crucified Christ. Above all, the Jews provided an outlet for aggressions the Poles could not completely release in their struggle against their Ukrainian neighbors.)

A wide pretentious staircase led to the apartments of the elite. It was always dirty because of the sizable traffic of clients and patients of the two lawyers and one doctor who lived on the upper floors. Another stairway was used by the water-carriers and the men who delivered the wood that was needed in massive quantities to make the fires in our large Dutch ovens burn continually day and night. The enormous fireplace in the kitchen was used for more than just cooking: here giant barrels of water stood ready for family washing, for scrubbing the kitchen and the other rooms, and, most important, for the children's Friday-night baths.

One-eyed Mr. Stein, the wood dealer, is standing before my eyes as he was on a certain hot, uneventful Sunday afternoon in my childhood. Nobody else was at home—I suppose this happened after my sisters were married. I was lying on the dining-room couch reading, enjoying my *dolce far niente,* practically naked except for a very light robe. Suddenly Mr. Stein appeared in the doorway without knocking, probably expecting that my mother would be at home to place her usual order. I jumped up and demanded angrily, "Mr. Stein, couldn't you knock first?" The answer was: "Why? Isn't this a Jewish house?" All the Jewish tradespeople we dealt with had this same feeling of solidarity with us despite the fact that we were members of the "aristocracy."

In one corner of the kitchen was a deep, well-built niche that was filled every morning with firewood. This dark hole was the home of the Witch. I lived in constant fear of her appetite, for Kasia, our remarkable cook, had told me that when the Witch was not satisfied with the kitchen scraps she ate up the children. It was a variation on the Hansel and Gretel story with a new, personal touch: I was at the time the only small child in the house.

Kasia . . . who would believe that this Polish farm woman who had never read a cookbook (she could scarcely read at all) and had never heard of French cuisine could produce such culinary masterpieces? Her pastries put to shame even the products of the local *Konditorei*, which was known throughout the region as one of the spots not to be missed in Przemyśl.

Among our next-door neighbors was the family of a small Jewish wine dealer. There were two children: one very fat boy a few years older than I, and a small daughter. My older sisters, Malvina and Gizela, used this neighbor boy once to play a cruel trick on me. They often released their aggressions on little Hala; I was my father's favorite and to them probably something of a spoiled baby. When Malvina's fiancé sent her a splendid bouquet after their formal engagement, my tormentors told me that it had been sent to *me*, by the fat boy. I wept bitterly, convinced that this bouquet made me his official fiancée and that I was now doomed to marry him someday. Adults who are not child psychologists may find such incidents humorous, not realizing that the tears might also be tragic. In this case my violent weeping may very well have been an indirect reaction to the approaching loss of Malvina.

I hardly knew the fat boy's little sister, but many years later when I was working at the Wagner-Jauregg Clinic in Vienna, supervising the admitting and releasing of chronically ill patients, her parents came to me in tears, begging me in the name of our former friendship not to allow their daughter to be sent to a mental institution for incurables.

Another apartment in the Gizowski house belonged to three lady teachers, already considered old maids. They had dedicated their lives to the care of their brother Józio, who was mentally retarded, an idiot who actually belonged in an institution. But since the establishments for the mentally ill in Poland had a bad reputation (except for private ones, which these poor teachers could not afford), Józio was kept at home and hung around the courtyard all day long. He was supposed to be harmless. When he had tantrums that seemed potentially dangerous, the sisters kept him locked up in their apartment.

For me, also idling around the courtyard, he was a permanent menace. Often we had to wait a long time outdoors in the freezing cold before getting into the toilet assigned to our apartment. Moreover the toilets had not been roofed over, and the partitions could be jumped over all too easily. Sometimes one had to linger in the toilet until Józio was through talking to himself and masturbating (his favorite activity) outside in the *pissoir*. I can't remember having any neurotic fears while I lived in that house; Józio provided enough real motivation for anxiety. When I think of the tender care that surrounded the children in our family, I wonder why my parents ignored this constant source of distress.

Another *Realangst* was the fear of encountering rats in the hallways and on the stairs, especially at night. Compared to these terrifying creatures, the legions of mice in our elegant apartment seemed harmless, and they led undisturbed, even comfortable lives. They took on a special significance for me after a short episode with my sisters in which I played a silent part: we were sitting in a room, Malvina and Gizela absorbed in some occupation or other, and I playing quietly. My sisters had a habit of speaking French when they had a conversation they didn't want me to hear. I can still see Malvina pointing to a mouse and murmuring: "Gizela, *regardez.*" It seemed obvious to me that she was speaking French so that the mouse wouldn't realize it had been seen. For many years I associated both the French language and mice with arcane and obscure matters, probably of a sexual nature.

I cannot omit from this list of characters Mrs. W., the dressmaker who lived on the third floor. (I have not tried to describe all the tenants of the Gizowski house, only those who still live in my memory as interesting or touching characters.) Mrs. W. always had a scarf tied around her head, as she was afflicted with migraine. She was our highest authority on fashions, the Christian Dior of Przemyśl. Every woman in the town with pretensions to elegance was dressed by Mrs. W.; when we sat on our balcony we could see the local society ladies going in and out. I was still too young to be a customer—that would come later—but since I had no friends in the house of my own age, and was often lonesome, I spent many hours with her, mostly playing under one of the worktables. Mrs. W. was not too pleased with this, but she never sent me away; I was, after all, a Rosenbach. I listened to the chatter of the seamstresses, who were usually bragging about their erotic conquests. One of them, I remember, had bulging "Basedow" eyes,[1] and she was convinced that they caught all men in their spell. I asked myself why no one had ever taken notice of *my* eyes. Mrs. W.'s son was one of the handsomest boys in the high school, but he had nothing to do with me. Platonic relationships were not for him. Old Mr. W. had been crippled by several strokes, and his wife had to support him. She never complained.

I've saved for last the most important resident of the Gizowski house: the boy who lived on the second floor, the hero of my erotic fantasies. There was a period when I told everyone who would listen to me, always under the seal of secrecy, that I was

1. Named after the doctor who discovered the connection between this phenomenon and thyroid hyperactivity (thyrotoxicosis).

having a torrid love affair with a young student. I described our rendezvous, the impassioned letters and poems he sent me, and the plans we had made for the future. It was all a complete fabrication, but I lived through it as though it were real, and besides I found it thrilling to describe it to other people as if it had happened. I waited at the window every evening to see him come home and then went off peacefully to bed. That was all the reality I needed to nourish my drama.

There was an attic in the Gizowski house where each apartment had its locked storage room. (Such rooms must exist all around the world; my friends in America have told me about finding in their attics sumptuous gowns left over from the days when women in their ball dresses looked like queens.) I knew every corner of the Gizowski attic but there was one I sedulously avoided. At the entrance, in the part of the attic that was not partitioned off into rooms, was a dimly lighted area where the adolescents of the house held actual orgies. I took no part in these and preferred my solitude, since at that time, in spite of my wicked reputation later, I was absolutely chaste. I never was a *demivierge,* as were almost all the girls I knew. I avoided completely even the innocent erotic games of adolescence.

I lived in the Gizowski house and in no other until I moved—or, rather, ran away—to Vienna in order to begin living a "free life." At that time, late adolescence, I wanted more than anything else to get away from home. I had an intense longing to understand and to take part in the great events of the world. It was not simply a craving for independence from my family.

Without meaning to, I became a pioneer in the town of Przemyśl. There were other girls who felt the same impulse that I had, yet didn't know how to carry it out, and my leaving home became a signal and an encouragement. Following my "demoralizing" example, six brave girls from good families brought themselves to the point of leaving their comfortable homes in the course of the next year.

There had been no talk, no propaganda. The other girls left

because my action had wakened in them the feeling that they could be free if they had the inner courage to revolt. How strange this must sound today, when young women have become liberated to such a degree! At that time we as girls had to struggle and sacrifice to achieve what is now taken for granted. The embattled gates to equal rights have indeed opened up for modern women, but I sometimes think to myself: "That is not what I meant by freedom—it is only 'social progress.' "

My parents moved into a house of their own on the river San after I was settled in Vienna, and I seldom visited them there. The new house was no substitute for the Gizowski place, which all my life has represented for me the lost paradise of childhood. I am glad that it was still standing when I brought Felix Deutsch into my family.

II

Father

I WAS BORN into a Polish-Jewish milieu at a time when the process of assimilation was in full swing. But the Jewish tendency to create a separate, closed, religious society within the larger society was also still operating. Caught in this conflict and ambiguity, I usually identified more with the romantic "suffering, enslaved Poland" than with my Jewish background. Anti-Semitism all around me tipped the scales further. In short, I wanted to be Polish. The influence of the budding Zionist nationalistic movement was not an important factor at the time of my childhood.

My father's social position helped to give me a sense of belonging in Polish society. Wilhelm Rosenbach was a prominent lawyer and a scholar in international law. He exerted considerable influence, especially after Galicia was granted a larger degree of autonomy within the Austro-Hungarian Empire and he was appointed to the important post of juridical representative of Galicia to the Federal Court in Vienna. (It was highly unusual to entrust such a great national responsibility to a Jew.) My father's law office in Przemyśl was a magnet for gifted young law students whose circumstances prevented them from studying at the universities of Kraków or Lwów. (Both universities had a long tradition of outstanding law professors.)

Father's office consisted of his own room and another one, small and dark, containing six desks and a crowd of clerks willing to take an unpaid job in this unpretentious office in order to have an opportunity to discuss cases with the great master of law. Since my father permitted me—his "Hala"—to stay in his office very often, and sit in a little chair under his enormous desk, I became familiar with a great variety of social problems. His clientele came from every rank of the society: Orthodox Jews, often very poor, sought his help in their clashes with the Polish aristocracy (*szlachta*); the aristocracy depended on the advice and wisdom of the Jewish lawyer in their permanent struggle with debts; the peasants appealed to my father for help against the power of their local *karczmarz*, the owner of the village inn where they brought their meager earnings to spend to the last penny on vodka.

These peasants regarded the innkeeper as the cause of their misery, and because he was almost invariably Jewish they extended their hate to Jews in general. They did not know that the real culprit was the aristocrat in his castle who levied heavy taxes on all the people, including the poor Jewish innkeeper, to pay the debts he ran up in order to maintain the illusion of his power and a pretentious life in the Parisian style.

My father's work widened my narrow middle-class environment in every direction, bringing me into contact with the rich, the poor, and the middle-class workers, too, in their endless struggle not to become proletarianized. But I benefited most of all from my father's professional and emotional ties with the inhabitants of the surrounding villages. My father often took me with him on his business visits to these villages, which were mostly Ruthenian, or Ukrainian.[1] To guard me from the winter frost he would stuff

1. This ethnic group was called Ruthenian by the Austrians and the Poles, and Ukrainian by its own leaders.

me into a fur-lined *fussack* that left only my face uncovered; in the summer, I would sit in his lap and from this vantage point look out over the villages with their meadows and ponds. I became very interested in the villagers and their way of life and on these visits learned a great deal of sociology firsthand. Although I was looking at their world from a comfortable two-horse carriage and heartily enjoyed my meals of fried eggs and thick cream, I was never unaware of the deep poverty of these grossly exploited peasants.

In a deep place in my heart I have kept the image of those humble thatched huts, each one monotonously like its neighbors, often with no chimney so that it was forever full of smoke, which could only escape through windows that never closed properly. A large part of such a hut served as a stable for the livestock, which was the family's chief source of nourishment and therefore was treated with special care. There the hired man lived together with the cows and horses.

Both the hired man and his master, the farmer, recognized only two earthly powers: the village priest, a delegate of the Almighty, and the Kaiser, represented by a man in uniform who appeared regularly to appropriate the farmer's last *groschen* for taxes or else recruit him into the slavery of military service. The Polish-Ukrainian peasant thought of the Kaiser quite literally as his own personal ruler, designated by God and himself nearly divine, who demanded service from his peasants but also took a direct interest in their many needs and problems.[1] He was next to God, the protector who gives freely and demands only what is necessary. The Polish and Ukrainian peasants were for centuries the most devoted and submissive element of the Austrian Empire. They obeyed without complaining, and when involved in legal wrangling with the local authorities they were convinced that if things went against them it was only because the Kaiser had not

1. I owe much of the information in this section to the writings of Jozef Wittlin, Professor Emeritus of Slavic Languages and Literatures at Harvard University.

been notified. If *he* were judging the case, he would be just, but he was simply too busy to take care of every one of his peasants personally. However, every peasant cherished the hope of meeting his emperor one day face to face and telling him about the bad management and injustice of his substitutes.

By extension, the *szlachcic* in his castle was also a semi-divine figure; he was almost as distant as the Kaiser, and had more important things to do than to care about Dmitry or Jacek. The priest was closer; he spoke with God in the church, yet in the churchyard he would ask each and every obscure member of his flock about his children and his cows, remind him of his sins, and offer redemption.

Helpless as this social order made him, the peasant remained capable of fighting for his rights. Sometimes he would be entangled in court procedures for years, watching his lost cause utterly absorb his hard-earned possessions. My father's role as lawyer for these naïve and fanatic peasants was often very frustrating; his effectiveness was limited by the obstinate attitudes of his clients.

This situation dominated the villages during my earliest childhood years. Later, enlightenment and organization were brought in by political organizers. Many years of education were needed to make the reactionary peasants conscious of the unreasonable conditions of their life, but eventually they were mobilized into a powerful mass resistance: they fought for the right to use meadows for pasture and waterways for their mills, and for their share of the forests. I stayed informed about these battles because of my father's position and my identification with him.

In my father's office I also learned about the host of smaller problems besetting the villagers. Unmarried mothers, for instance, were a common occurrence. The problem had nothing to do with morality, sometimes involved love, but usually was a matter to be resolved by some kind of financial reparation. The girls I saw in the office frequently named the local landowner as the father; he seldom denied it and usually left the affair for his lawyer to settle. All this was quite an education for a little girl!

The position of my family and the respect paid to my father by all classes in the community provided me with a certain degree of inoculation against the stigma of being Jewish. But it was unavoidably plain to me that in their struggle against exploitation the peasants made the Jew their scapegoat. He was conceived of as a type of devil who sucked away their savings for his own advantage. Often the Jew was indeed the immediate exploiter, but behind him stood the peasants' own near-deity, the aristocratic *szlachcic*. For instance, very often a Jewish lumber dealer—and there were many of them—had to pay the *Pan* (a term for the *szlachcic* used by his social inferiors) an exorbitant price for his wood plus an extra charge for permission to cut it. This forced the Jewish dealer to charge a high price for the lumber. Here the peasant and the Jew were fellow victims. But, trapped in this chain of social misery, the peasant could be easily convinced that the Jews were to blame for all the evils of his life.

One should not forget that the peasant, usually illiterate, took his religious ideas whole-cloth from the village priest, a figure of enormous influence, whose interpretation of the New Testament was laced with literal-minded bigotry. Every Sunday the flock was vigorously reminded that it was the Jews who crucified Christ.

For their part, the Jews in their need often took advantage of the peasants' stupidity. I myself have watched scenes that despite their tragic undertones could have come straight out of a vaudeville act. I could tell many stories like the following:

Every sizable village had its market day when the farmers brought their produce in to barter for clothing, linen, and other necessities. At one of these markets, I saw a peasant trying on an odd-looking hat, unable to decide whether to buy it. All at once the Jewish peddler began to yell, "Michal! Michal!" "But I'm right here!" exclaimed the prospective buyer in surprise, to which the Jew replied, "Ah, of course, of course . . . but how could I have guessed that this distinguished-looking man with the fine hat could possibly be that poor farmer Michał?"

Such were the petty revenges of humor. But in fact there was little room in Polish society for the Jew, for this poor figure bent by prayers and apprehension, with little pride in his existence, persecuted not only in the annals of the past but every day. In Przemyśl I often witnessed Gentile boys throwing stones and urging their dogs to chase and bark at "the Jew" or even to bite him. It was not the Jew's proverbial inherited anxiety that made him run, it was the actual dangers he faced daily.

I must confess with shame that I learned the Jewish melody of the Hora, a song of joy, not from groups of Jews dancing and singing but as a satirical song that Christian boys sang on the streets of Przemyśl. *"Hey ty zydku, hoira, hoira, czemu tobie moira, moira?"* ("Hey, you little Jew, hoira, hoira, what do you have to fear, to fear?") This melody runs through my life as a memento and an appeal to my identity. I have to make a further confession: I was furious but helpless against the Catholic boys, and I was deeply ashamed of my connection with the wildly running, panicking Jews. Did I sing along with the boys in order to prove I was not one of "them"?

There is another memory: sitting by the window of my sister's house in Strzyzów on moonlit evenings and watching the ortho-dox Jews of the neighborhood gather to pray in the open air. Why didn't these ceremonies evoke any reverence in the on-lookers? And why not in me, so easily moved to ecstasy?

I know I felt that being my father's daughter placed me in a special category, despite my Jewishness. This may be the reason why being Jewish has never, since my childhood, made me feel really inferior.

Because of my unusually constant companionship with Father in those early years, it was natural that I was often immersed in fantasies connected with him. One of these is so typical that it has acquired a name in psychoanalytic literature. It is called the "family romance" and has many variations. In some of mine my father was debased, in others elevated. The debased father was personified by Fedko Lachyta—the real name of one of my father's clients—and I have a vague feeling that my older sisters, probably jealous of Father's love for me, once told me that this dirty farmer was my real father, from whom Father bought me because he was in love with me. (I suppose that the last part of the story was added by me.)

Another "family romance" of mine was more elevated but also much more realistic. Here my real father was a very elegant aristocrat who was often a guest in my parents' house. I was supposed to be the product of my mother's infidelity. Whereas the Fedko Lachyta story debased both my parents into illiterate peasants, the second romance accepted the identity of my mother and endowed me with an upper-class, non-Jewish father.

A different group of fantasies centered around my actual physical birth. As I remember, the usual lies of grownups—the stork story, the market where children are bought, the angel who brings them from heaven, etc.—were completely rejected, as they usually are. I had a period of great preoccupation with the subject, but the typical questions about my mother's pregnancy, the usual curiosity about and investigation of her body, and the evidence of a "primal scene" did not appear in my early childhood, but later on in preadolescence, already intellectualized. Of course, by the time fairy tales started to nourish my fantasies, Cinderella was my definite favorite. I was myself a third daughter and the idea of being loved by my father and hated by my mother was nothing new to me. The "bad sisters" were secondary characters for me; by preadolescence they had changed into my allies against the bad mother. In my earliest fantasies, even those concerning my birth, I was attempting to minimize her importance in my life. My wish not to have been born to her was dramatized in a daydream associating with my birth only Mrs. G., the short fat midwife who assisted women of "good" Jewish society. Later on it was sometimes my father who, at my demand, took over the activities usually assigned to the mother, such as carrying and feeding me. And certain experiences of *déjà vu* related to my earliest childhood were intended to prove (to myself) that I never was a helpless little baby completely dependent on my mother.

The true facts of my birth turned into a family saga, which I probably heard often and embellished with my own embroidery. But it is clear that long before I was born my family had already stigmatized my life with vain expectations. They wished to have a son, after having two girls and a boy, Emil, who to their disappointment had not turned out as they wished. They wanted a real "heir" who would follow in his father's footsteps and be pointed out by others as "his father's son." Emil even in his first years in school had not shown the least trace of his father's intellect and character; he gave no promise of fulfilling his Jewish parents' most vital wish: to have a great man for a son. This wish is shared by most Jewish families, and its origin is hidden far back in the history of the race. Emil's burden as the only son was made heavier by the fact that he had a prominent man for a father and was obliged to do as well or better.

His school reports were dismal, so my father decided, following a well-known Jewish joke,[1] to let Emil be baptized. Only in this way would he be able to make a career for himself in civil service, with the help of my father's connections. Accordingly Emil was baptized and made his career, later marrying the daughter of a Polish general. Nobody ever said of him, "He's just like old Rosenbach." That remark was reserved for someone who was, as it happened, only a girl.

When I was born, Malvina was eleven, Gizela seven, and Emil ten. The great gap between our ages made me in effect an only child. They must have been jealous of me from the beginning; in later years I was jealous of *them,* as I waited impatiently to grow up.

My father was away on a business trip when I came into the world, and when on his return the midwife presented him with his newborn child it must have been a terrible blow to find he had a third daughter. However, as the saga goes, even before he

---

1. Little Moritz brings home a poor report card. Called in to explain it to his parents, he protests: "It's because the teacher is an anti-Semite." So they let him be baptized; but Moritz's next report card is no better. His parents once again demand an explanation. This time he shrugs, "It's just because we Gentiles are pretty dumb."

knew whether the baby was boy or girl, he had already fallen in love with the large radiant eyes looking up at him. (I suppose that this was a transference of interest from an organ that might disappoint him to another feature that unquestionably pleased him, no matter what the child's sex.) For many years his enchantment persisted. He was devoted to me and accepted me fully, not as a substitute for a boy but as his spiritual heir as well as his beloved girl with the beautiful eyes. I was endowed with the qualities of "old Rosenbach," regardless of my sex.

I know little about the first five years of my life. The story goes that I had nine different nurses, suffered from a chronic intestinal catarrh, and in spite of all my fretting remained my father's darling. My mother looked after my health and cleanliness with cool efficiency. Later on she used to say that my stormy and turbulent life could be traced back to my having had nine nurses.

Unless I went to his office, I seldom saw my father during the day. At suppertime he would come directly from the office to the dining-room table carrying a bottle of wine or cognac from the locked iron liquor closet. He would try to keep from giving me his whole attention, but I always had the feeling that we shared a secret.

In his youth, Father had a great many interests outside of his profession, but his work gradually came to occupy most of his time. Only his love of music survived, and this had the greatest effect on me. From my childhood on, it was a bond between us. I remember best the easier tunes he shared with me, such as Johann Strauss' "Die Fledermaus" and Offenbach's "Die Schöne Helena." He used to sing these to me with slight changes in the lyrics, such as, "Die Hala mit der Rute schlagen, das ist gegen mein Prinzip, zip, zip, zip, zip . . ." ("It is against my principles to strike my Hala with the rod, zip. . . .")

My favorite composer when I was a girl was, of course, Chopin; later his place was taken by Mozart and Beethoven. Records did not exist as yet, but our piano was good, and quite talented young musicians came to play in our salon. Both my sisters played the piano, and I might have too if a seemingly trivial incident had not brought my musical expression to an abrupt and sad end. This is what happened:

There were some good female music teachers in Przemyśl but only one man, who had become more or less a must for the children of "the right people." All Rosenbach children went through the mill of his teaching, but only Gizela found him helpful. She had not only talent but a sweet passive personality. I think that in a society where women's talents were taken seriously, Gizela would have developed into a real musician. Unfortunately, like Malvina with her painting, Gizela had to restrict herself to a ladylike, amateur use of her talent. My own lessons were a torture for me and a nuisance for Professor G. The piano stood, according to custom, in the big cold salon with its highly polished floor. One day during my lesson, my mother was passing through and slipped and fell on the mirror-like surface. Since she was stout and quite heavy, she couldn't get back on her feet unaided; there she lay on her back, marooned. I found this view of her hilarious, and instead of springing up to help her, I stayed where I was, laughing hysterically. My teacher jumped to his feet, roaring, "This is no child, it's a wild animal! I'll never teach her again!"

From that time on I shunned the piano with a kind of phobia. I can't remember with any certainty what effect the incident had on my relationship with Father, but I know that little by little he transferred his encouragement from me to Gizela, the really musical one. However, it was his strong and lasting influence that enabled me to appreciate fully the music Vienna offered me during my student years. To be sure, the cultural atmosphere of Vienna was also responsible, and the fact that with little money and plenty of enthusiasm one could participate in great moments in the world of art. I remember waiting up all night with other students, on our tiny folding stools, to buy standing-room tickets for the following evening's opera.

But it was my husband's great, creative musicianship that brought back my musical interests after years of stagnation. Until this revival I had deprived myself of the pleasure of playing the piano, doubtless as an unconscious self-punishment for sadistic feelings against my mother. My analytic experience with patients has shown me how easily artistic gifts can be blighted by neurosis; sometimes merely one isolated traumatic experience can cause permanent damage.

As I look back over what I have written so far, I can see clearly a pervading emotional bias: the experiences are set down truthfully but the negative elements are often omitted. This is especially true vis-à-vis my relationship with my father. Certain intensely felt experiences, which could have formed the kernel of a neurosis in childhood but didn't, have not been adequately explored. Also, a high degree of ambivalence toward my father, which I can only vaguely trace out, has been buried under the impact of the great love that bound us together. I now realize that I exploited tyrannically my father's passivity, which I was painfully aware of in his relationship to my mother. Yet so far I have avoided mentioning this crucial factor.

A few fragments remain from a childhood neurosis that manifested itself in a terrible fear not *of* him but *for* him. My father spent most of his evenings at his club, where the leading men of the town met to play cards. He usually came home fairly late. I remember waiting anxiously for his return; unable to fall asleep, I would sit on the windowsill staring at the street corner and listening to every sound with intense apprehension. My fears were horrible: from my window I saw threatening figures lying in wait to murder him. As soon as I spied him coming around the corner, I would slip back into bed and pretend to be asleep. By the time he passed my bed, carrying the lamp in his hand, my anxiety would have vanished completely.

Throughout my life I have been free of neuroses concerning my own safety, but my childhood anxiety for my father has been echoed and re-echoed in later phobic fears, especially for my older grandson Peter.

When I was still fairly young, though several years into school life, my parents planned a trip to Switzerland, naturally without the "little one." I sat in a corner secretly reading Aunt Frania's Baedeker of Switzerland. One day they discovered me with the book and asked how I knew about the trip. I replied something like, "Oh, everyone knows about it." The period before their departure is quite confused in my memory, but I have the feeling I tried very hard to appear nonchalant. I was left in the care of the old-maid principal of the private school I had attended during my first school years, someone I had disliked from the first.

My parents came back with an extraordinarily beautiful doll for me. She could close her eyes, walk on her two stiff legs, etc. She was like a real child. At this time I had no playmates and not enough uninhibited fantasy to imagine a satisfying relationship with my beautiful doll. So I just played mother, ardently and spasmodically, and after a time abandoned the doll and refused to have another, which seems to me very significant. My relationship to my father was changing drastically. He had started to turn his attention more and more toward my two older sisters; and though he brought me home a beautiful doll, he had abandoned me and deprived me of his companionship when he went to Switzerland with the rest of the family. So I abandoned my doll— after treating it as my own child.

Many episodes illustrating my early relationship with Father were remembered for years by witnesses outside the family. One in particular points up the preadolescent ambiguity of my feelings. On Sundays my mother used to take advantage of my father's freedom from his work and leave me in his care. We would go for a stroll, with me hanging proudly on his hand; lots of men would greet us, smiling at me. Almost every Sunday we would meet a friend of Father's whose name has stuck in my memory because of its inappropriateness. He was called Smutny, which means "the sad man," but was one of the cheeriest people I knew. The name may also have stuck in my memory because of his connection with an episode he recalled to me many years later in Vienna. Mr. Smutny came to the city to consult Professor Wagner-Jauregg about a relative. I was already an experienced psychiatrist and since Mr. S. was Polish he was referred to me, but as soon as he heard my name he cried out in mock horror, "I, go to that stubborn brat? Never!" He was referring to a long-ago Sunday when he had tried to join Father and me on our walk and I had thrown a monumental tantrum that left my father helpless: I stood as if nailed to the street and spurned all efforts to make me budge. I wouldn't let Father carry me or run with me down the street. I don't remember how it all came out, but now I can see one clear meaning of that scene: I wanted to have Father to myself!

On another level this childish outburst was, I think, a part of my war for independence, which began long before my adolescence. There was something within me that demanded a loosening of the bonds between my father and me—a normal psychobiological process that from time to time loudly clamored for its rights. The conflict is obvious: I didn't want to share my father's attention, yet even while I indirectly demanded to be carried by him, I stubbornly refused to be carried. Like other children, I probably really wanted to run aimlessly away from him and turn into a "big girl." Somewhat later, in adolescence, I actually made such flights.

The uncalculated preadolescent outburst had no other purpose than to give vent to growing inner unrest. Characteristically, during the Smutny episode I automatically retreated to my earlier position of security as a defense, though it actually was the very danger from which I wanted to flee!

Around that time or somewhat later I began to read voraciously, first under the influence of my Aunt Frania and then stimulated by the arrival of a governess, Mademoiselle Deux (that was her real name). Though beginning with children's books, I was soon absorbed in Polish poetry and books of all kinds in several languages. I had a great talent for learning new languages at that time, which I later lost, apparently for psychological reasons. Father took no active interest in my education, yet he had the greatest influence on it of all. For instance, he would read Goethe to me even in the time before I could read myself. He was continually reciting Schiller for his own pleasure; this inspired in me a passion to be an actress, which soon died out, but also left me with a love for Schiller that was lasting.

Father cared very little about our religious or spiritual development, though he was indeed a respected figure in the Jewish religious community and its legal representative, in spite of the active role he played in Polish society.[1] His influence on us was indirect; the strength of his character operated as an example, especially on me. For a long time he remained the model for my ego-ideal. During my college years, two of my girlfriends and I were in the vanguard of the battle to get permission for women to study law at the University of Vienna. It was our stubborn demands that won this victory for women.[2] I was motivated by the ideology of equal rights for all, not by a personal interest in the law. (For a brief period I had aspired to become a colleague of my father, but that wish had been given up years before.) Yet I am sure that identification with my father was my deepest motive for this campaign.

His influence did not grow out of inspiring talk or even impressive deeds; it was the minor everyday incidents that left their mark on me. For instance, it seems to me I was exposed to the essence of democracy in the way he handled the small cases that made up the bulk of his daily work. As I have said, his office was the meeting point of various social classes. Sheltered under his big desk, I could see him throwing open his office doors and calling out, "Next!" Naturally if one of his aristocratic clients were waiting outside, that man would rise self-importantly from

1. I still have the two beautiful silver candelabras of delicate Italian workmanship given to my father as a token of gratitude by the Jewish community in Przemyśl.

2. Our method of fighting was to stand every morning before the door of the minister who directed the law school, until we had forced him to agree to act on our demands. Incidentally, immediately after this achievement, one of our trio suddenly withdrew, leaving us in order to marry a handsome Hussar.

his seat. But Father would turn toward a poor peasant, asking, "Weren't *you* here first?" The *szlachcic* would be infuriated, the peasant astonished, and I am sure that the effect on me, however unconscious, emerged later during my political activities. Father's influence came from his personality, from the way he lived.

There were times during my adolescence when my father ceased to be my ally as he had been during childhood. During my mother's reactionary counterattacks on my efforts to liberate myself he was often on the enemy side. Perhaps the Bobniszcze episode was the turning point in our close relationship.

There was a family in Przemyśl with three sons who were very well spoken of, and deservedly so. One of the young men was a gifted mathematician who, if I remember rightly, spent most of his life in Vienna, first as a student and later as a teacher. Another brother was active in my father's office as an apprentice lawyer. Since I always had free access to the office and my father was often out, this young man and I became warm friends. Through him I met his mathematician brother, an ascetic idealist, fanatically devoted to progressive ideas, who took an active interest in my struggle for personal freedom. Once he brought a woman friend home to meet his parents, and also introduced her to me. I believe she had already completed her medical studies. I don't know what became of her later, but on this visit I had an opportunity to be with people who were fighting not just for their personal freedom but for an ideal of freedom for all men and women. The two of them took me on an excursion to a place with a name that is stamped on my memory because it is so unusual. It is called Bobniszcze and it was famous for its caverns. We spent the night in one of the caverns and early next morning walked the long dusty road to the nearest railroad station. And there at the station was my father, accompanied by a pair of gendarmes, to save his daughter from the clutches of immoral seducers!

And yet even now I still have the feeling that at the bottom of his heart my father really belonged to "our world," but felt bound to carry out my mother's instructions. I was hurt by this, but it never occurred to me that he could have opposed her if he wished. I enjoyed too much my theory that we were both her victims. Father was a brave man, and feared only two people: my mother (with reason), and his obstinate darling. Only now can I understand how his conflicting emotions helped cause his often contradictory behavior to me.

I never actually abdicated my position as the heir of "old Rosenbach" but I was a generation younger than he, and waging a war of personal independence. Indulgence in the aura of fatherly love that always surrounded me definitely had to be subordinated, if not given up. That is the task of every normal adolescent not hindered by neurosis: to free himself from the emotional dependencies of childhood. By the time of the Bobniscze episode, I had already acquired some measure of self-confidence, but it was the drama at the railroad station that finally dissolved my dependence on Father. I still wanted to have him as an ally, though, and I remember that he too seemed to have this ambivalent attitude. But after this episode, he threw himself even more intensely into his professional world and, to my sisters' delight, no longer allowed me to enter his office any time I wished. This seemingly unkind behavior was justified by its results—it gave me the final push to grow up emotionally. Psychological growth was also furthered by the fact that in this difficult period I was fairly alone. By this time both my sister Malvina and my Aunt Frania were married and had their own personal problems to deal with.

To look backward a bit from the Bobniszcze affair: the whole course of my liberation was beset with difficulties. The spirit of revolution was always in me, but at first it had no more concrete goal than: "*Something's* got to happen!" I believe that my father also found himself in a dilemma. He was no longer able to protect me from real experience of the outside world by hiding me under his tall desk, yet he obviously feared the dangers that might threaten me. In his view, I wasn't yet entitled to the rights of a grown-up daughter. He still regarded me as his little girl, but I had begun to find my protected life meaningless.

Since 1964 I have taken an active interest in the psychology of adolescence. In my book on this subject[1] I actually had less to say about feminine than masculine adolescent problems. But I gave marked attention to one feminine type in particular: the daughter who adopts her father's ideals and fights on his behalf, along with him, for these goals. The girl of this type builds her life upon her identification with her father. I was of course such a girl. My adolescence coincided, however, with political upheavals that came to their climax in the anti-Czarist Russian Revolution. New ideals were injected into Polish society that destroyed the lifeline between my father's generation and my own. As soon as Father aggressively opposed my modern crusade for freedom, for instance in the Bobniszcze episode, a whole epoch of my life came to an end.

As I write this autobiography I realize that there were years during my adolescence when my father virtually disappeared from my sphere of interests. I see clearly now that my love relationship (perhaps premature) with the Socialist leader Herman Lieberman,[2] a man much older than I, was so much a father-transference that my love for Father was weakened. During this time my father was totally wrapped up in his work, and his interests were no longer in harmony with my sublimation of energies into politics and medical school.

Destiny provided an epilogue to our relationship. World War I brought us together again temporarily, for my entire family spent the war years in Vienna. Together we followed the fortunes of our native town. "Przemyśl is still ours" meant almost as much to us as "All quiet on the western front" in Remarque's novel. And one of the brightest moments for me in this dark time was the fact that my father was able to meet Felix and come to love him.

1. *Selected Problems of Adolescence: With Special Emphasis on Group Formation,* Monograph Series of The Psychoanalytic Study of the Child, no. 3 (New York: International Universities Press, 1967).
2. Hereafter referred to as L.

My family left for home as soon as the war's end permitted. They were already gone when my child was born, and I could not immediately fulfill my father's burning wish to see my little son, as travel to Poland was extremely difficult even after the formal declaration of peace. But eventually Father did see the son of his dear Hala; this meeting was a loving gift of fate.

When my father returned to Przemyśl, he resumed his professional work in his old office. Unfortunately old age and his weak heart interrupted this attempt before long. He died suddenly, and according to the family saga had in the meantime lost all of his hard-earned property, apparently through his own fault. I am glad that his death spared him the Nazi occupation of Przemyśl. I own photographs recording the Nazis' establishment of a ghetto in Przemyśl and I know the history of their persecution of its inhabitants, including many of those I loved. I often ask myself: did I do all I could to help?

III

Sisters

D U R I N G this autobiographical writing more and more
memories emerge from the amnesia that seemed, during my
psychoanalysis, to have buried deeply the first five years of my
life. Little incidents that took place in my fifth year indicate
strict control by the superego. My sister Malvina played a large
role in the formation of this superego, even though I identified
with my father from early childhood.

My mother, with her wild, uncontrollable outbreaks of temper,
often directed against me, represented a terrifying external force
against which I was totally helpless. I see Malvina as my "good"
mother and the savior of my femininity, endangered by the
absence of any favorable identification with my real mother.

Malvina, whom I idolized, was for me the highest authority:
fate had invested her with the right to punish and to pardon.
Even my toilet training, a difficult task with any child, was part
of her duties. Thus it happened that she—herself little more than
a child, maybe fourteen or fifteen—would often be waked up in
the night to set me on the "potty" or to hear an anguished cry,

"Lincia, I can't sleep, I've done something bad." The sin was not described in words but had to do with sitting longer than was necessary for the bowel movement and feeling guilty about the masturbatory pleasure associated with this function. I might add that in spite of the anality evident in these episodes, I escaped the danger of developing an "anal personality."

Malvina's influence became less direct after she married and moved to another town—I was ten at the time. But in my years of latency and early puberty she was an object of identification and my superego built itself around her ways.

She seemed to be the incarnation of goodness. She never passed a beggar (there were many of them in the streets of Przemyśl, especially around the churches) without giving him something out of her modest savings. On certain fixed days of the week all sorts of misshapen creatures would gather outside the kitchen door: for instance, Karolinchen, who wandered from house to house wearing the rags of a black velvet dress and matching hat, leaving behind her a penetrating smell because she obviously never bathed. She always asked for a few coins to buy a bit of cream; sometimes we would also set aside a little milk to fill her chipped pitcher. When asked where she came from, she would become loquacious and tell us stories about the diamonds and pearls in the court of her royal parents. Malvina could never be wholly convinced that these were merely Karolinchen's delusions. "There must be *some* truth in it," she would say. And she would often walk arm in arm with Karolinchen, to discourage the boys in the street from taunting and throwing stones at her, as they often did when she was alone.

I could fill a large psychiatric ward with Malvina's protégés. There was something so human and at the same time godlike about her sympathy for the suffering pariahs she took under her wing that the townspeople of Przemyśl called her "holy Malvina" without irony.

The demands she made on herself amounted to an asceticism that sometimes took on bizarre forms. She was forever washing her hands, for instance, and sucking her fingernails in a grotesque way in order to clean them. Much later, as a psychiatrist, I realized that Malvina suffered from a compulsion neurosis, expressed not only in her personality structure but in outward symptoms too. She was a compulsive talker and would often ask, "Do you see what I mean?," repeating several times what she had just said, in visible fear of not being understood. People liked her, but frequently avoided her.

I began at an early age to imitate Malvina; when I was ten I began to visit the houses of the poor. Poland was full of them. The small packages I handed out, filled with the cheapest kind of food, were received with a mixture of gratitude and bitter amusement at the comedy being acted out by the little rich girl. And it was a comedy. Yet this direct encounter with social injustice was perhaps one of the root causes of my adolescent sympathy with the Socialist Party. And *that* was genuine, in spite of my youth.

Malvina was beautiful, elegant, and well-bred. She had a great talent for painting, which, if it had been encouraged, might have turned her into a serious artist. But in our social milieu, who cared about the talents of a mere girl? The same indifference let Gizela's musical gift go to waste.

Malvina's later life was a chain of tragedy, twisted by neurosis and my mother's domination, though it was not without its romance. I myself reacted to the events of her life with an intuitive sense of frustration that she was not handling them as I would have in her place. This is not a projection of later feelings back into childhood; I am sure that my memory of Malvina's difficulties is very clear. There was something already growing within me then, the first sprouts of objectivity and rebellion that helped me shake off my oldest sister's obsessive-neurotic influence. In my continual struggle with my mother, this same antagonistic reaction proved a strong ally in my war for freedom.

When Malvina was eighteen and I was seven, her ascetic mode of life came to a turbulent end. I had already begun to turn away from her compulsive orbit and was becoming a normal little girl. The implicit animosity between Malvina and my mother finally came into the open when my mother began to insist dogmatically that any unmarried girl older than eighteen was an old maid, and she would never tolerate this in *her* family. Poor Malvina was forced to marry. She was to be allowed to choose her own husband, but within limits. Naturally, the young man had to meet certain standards required by our family's social position: he must come from a good Jewish family and hold a job suited to his social class, that is, he had to be in a position to establish and support a family. What a difference in marriage customs between then and now! When I was young, it was not unusual for the groom to be eight or ten years older than the bride. Also, it was taken for granted that the bride would have a dowry. The usual marriage occurred after deliberate calculations: "He is worth so much, she will bring so much; all right, they can get married." A marriage contracted without a dowry was considered a pure "love match."

Along with a common culutral background, a marriage would be the result of acquaintance, with or without love, or the efforts of friends and busybodies. I have the impression that middle-aged Jewish ladies played the game of matchmaking with passionate zeal. The institution of the *Schadchen* (matchmaker), once popular in Jewish circles, was by my time largely outmoded in Poland and hardly existed in our milieu, though the Schadchen's own conviction that Jewish marriages could not be brought about properly without his help and his aggressive battle for survival kept him an active, typical figure in the small provincial towns.

Actually we were paid visits by one of these shabby figures, who appeared uninvited at the back door, to the amazement of our snobbish kitchen staff. I would run away in fright whenever I saw the ugly figure slink into view. He had with him a list of likely prospects, chosen mainly for their financial qualifications. I later heard this story about his visit, supposed to be true: when the

Schadchen presented my mother with a list of candidates, she declared, in an effort to get rid of him, that her daughter could marry no one less than a prince, whereupon he triumphantly replied, "I have one of those too!"

We younger children of course had no idea how big our sister's dowry was. But I know that my father's position counted for a lot. It had to —he was never a wealthy man.

Malvina in the meantime was waiting with an uneasy heart for a great love—and it came! Romantic, passionate, happy—but forbidden! He was an officer in the Austrian army, distinguished and well brought up, but, alas, a Christian. These officers were well-known for their anti-Semitism, but often married Jewish girls for their dowries, because of a military law requiring every officer who got married to have a certain sum of money at his disposal, his so-called *Kaution*. In many cases, an officer could pay his debts only by marrying a girl with a large dowry. In Malvina's case, however, it was true love, and neither my father nor my mother said no to the marriage. It was Grandfather Leizor (my mother's father and a hypocrite we all despised) whose veto destroyed the happiness of two deserving young people. Social progress and more liberal attitudes have not completely rooted out such Jewish family traditions. Even today one can see Grandfather Leizors ruining young lives with their aggressive spite.

I can still see clearly across eighty years a heroic Malvina saying farewell to her beloved. It was a cold winter day, it was snowing, and I, barely eight years old, was standing by the glass front door waiting for our servant Jacek to return. He was taking a long time buying cigarettes for the household. In the salon were my parents, Malvina, and the young officer. The atmosphere was laden with tension and nobody had any time for a forlorn little girl. I believe that I knew very well what was going on, and that with all my child's heart I was on the side of the lovers. Jacek came back, drunk, but the young officer disappeared forever.

The only false note I can find in this memory is the glass door. There was no glass door in my parents' house. It has been borrowed from my present home. My husband and I had it installed so that we could enjoy more fully and calmly the time of homecoming after work. The loneliness of my present life and my ceaseless mourning for my husband are visibly influencing the associative course of my memories. My deeply rooted identification with Malvina has fused my loss and hers into one, and this fusion is expressed in the merging of two distinct places—as so often happens in our dreams.

To return to Malvina's story: by the time she reached twenty-one, her grief seemed to have quieted down, and my mother began once more to press for a marriage. She was visibly in a panic of fear that her daughter would be an old maid, and twenty-one was a signal that such a catastrophe was at hand. A new round of torture began for Malvina, as my mother's impatience to marry her off became very aggressive. The psychological reasons for this intensity are not clear to me.

Mutual friends introduced Malvina to a man who himself was nearly past what is considered the marriageable prime. Jacob was not a small-town type, but necessity had forced him to establish his law practice in Rzeszow, a small *Städtle* near Krakow. He was a man of great elegance, good-looking, and proud. Malvina fell passionately in love with him at their very first meeting.

After a courtship of several months Malvina and Jacob became engaged, and during the period between the engagement and the wedding Jacob came from Rzeszow on weekends to visit us. Paradoxically, I don't remember much about these visits except for some small, indirect actions of mine that reveal my intense jealousy. For instance, I recall a scene in which I embarrassed the whole family. During an abundant and elegantly served luncheon I began to protest that I hadn't been given enough cucumber salad, and loudly complained that we never had it at all unless we had a guest. Naturally nobody suspected that this unusual behavior was a child's reaction to a feeling of deep loss.

Malvina's wedding was our cook Kasia's most brilliant triumph: "everybody" was there. They all came to show respect for my father, and for my mother it was a pinnacle of social recognition. But Kasia's glory was undeniable; everyone knew that she alone had prepared the culinary orgy for one hundred guests.

The bride sat at her wedding with eyes red from weeping, and Jacob retreated into his own depression. For me, in spite of the delicious food, it was in effect Malvina's funeral. There is a Polish saying: *"Kiedy na dziewczynę zawołają żono, już ją żywcem pogrzebiono."* ("When a girl becomes a wife, she is buried alive.") I certainly felt that way, and so (I believe) did Malvina. When the men came for her trunk on the following day, I wailed in complete despair, "They're taking Malvina away!"

The next few years of my life remain relatively obscure to me. To whom could my isolated heart turn? There was my Aunt Frania, who became my lifesaver; there were my three cousins, who were friendly; and there were some older schoolgirls from the country who boarded with an old widow on the fourth floor and refused to let me into their circle. I felt very lonely, especially after Uncle R. and his wife, "the beautiful Helena"—a younger sister of my mother after whom I had been named—and their three children, my beloved cousins, moved away to the smaller town of Stryj.

The summers I spent in Stryj with them became my true life; in between there was school, boredom, fantasy-making. In Stryj we went around with the students and had small, harmless romances that served merely to give some content to our conversations about love. It was at this time that I developed a mythical love experience, as described in an earlier chapter, which I recounted dramatically to my cousins, complete with secret rendezvous and erotic scenes. I now see that this was the forerunner of my later tendency to fantasize ("pseudologia phantastica"). In my analysis I traced these fabrications (which my friends believed and which gave me the reputation of a "fallen woman") to an actual attempt by my brother to seduce me.

The coming-on of femininity made itself felt during my first visits to Malvina in her new home. Her ground-floor apartment faced the local high school, and I spent much of my time watching the students come and go. From time to time one of them would bestow on me a passing interest. But for the students I was still a child, without any physical attraction to speak of. On the whole I was more interested in Malvina's honeymoon and the erotic sphere of her new marriage than in my own physical development. After Malvina became pregnant she began to withdraw into her own inner world. My visits became less and less frequent and I was again isolated in my loneliness.

I have the feeling that Malvina's departure was not the only reason for the sense of impoverishment I felt at this time. My other sister, Gizela, whom I had always liked very much, might have filled for me the gap left by Malvina. But she was also feeling the loss of a close companion, and reacted by intensifying her friendships with girls of her own age, especially Irene, who lived on the fourth floor—a temperamental, clever girl with two very good-looking brothers. There was also Kazia, daughter of the poor widow B. on the second floor. Above all, Gizela had her admiring circle of students, who had always been more interested in her than in the lovely but proud Malvina. I still remember the ending of one of many poems Gizela received in love letters: *"Przeszkoczyłbym ja ganeczek za twój Giziu calusezek."* ("I'd even climb up to a balcony for one little kiss from Gizela.")

It astounds me how precise my memory is of these seemingly unimportant details. I suspect that they became important because they were woven into my own fantasies. In any case, my identification with Malvina's sadness outweighed and left a deeper impression than any empathy with Gizela in her happiness. Whenever Gizela played the piano (Ravel's *Bolero* was my favorite piece) I would lie on the floor and weep a flood of tears.

The intimacy between my two older sisters had very often made me feel like Cinderella. As I have said earlier, they would sit together speaking French; and to this day I still have the feeling that foreign languages serve as a disguise for forbidden secrets. I myself have grown away from my mother tongue, and yet my pronunciation in every language remains Polish In the long run we react instinctively in the language of our childhood. When I'm oppressed by personal sorrows, I exhort myself with these words of Słowacki: *"Nie czas załować róż gdy płoną lasy."* ("No time to cry over roses when forests are burning.") Or when I must point out to a narcissistically inflated "friend" the meanness of his behavior, I say, *"Ptak ptakowi nie dorówna nie poleci orzeł w gówna."* ("One bird is not like another—an eagle will never fly to dung.")

Malvina and Gizela spoke French intermittently in the presence of myself and the mice. (Being Polish mice, they would not gather that they were being observed!) My sisters also instantly broke into that other language whenever Jacek, the manservant, appeared. A prying type, Jacek had a genius for small vulgarities that fell just short of obscenity, and it was he who applied himself with much success to encourage my narcissism, which was hyperactive during those years. The greatest compliment he would use to corrupt me was that legions of men would kill themselves for love of me. This prophecy gave me a kind of phobia that for some time took all the pleasure out of being loved. I was so afraid of its coming true that when my cousin Lolo came to visit us in Przemyśl and, as he was leaving, drew me aside to give me a letter that began, "When you read these lines I will no longer be among the living," I saw it as direct confirmation of Jacek's prediction. Soon after, I learned that Lolo had not committed suicide at all.

Other small episodes of a harmless nature produced exaggerated guilt reactions and expectations of catastrophe in me. Jacek's foolish prophecy became a *memento mori*. Evidently it served me as a defense mechanism—an excuse to avoid the emotional perils of love. Once when I was fourteen, my mother took me along with her on a trip to Lwów, where we stayed at a very elegant hotel. The romantic setting itself must have stimulated the fantasies of a young student who followed us everywhere, as a young man in

love is proverbially supposed to do. In the evening I found a
letter addressed to me at the hotel desk. I didn't dare to open it
for fear that it was a suicide note, and all night long I thought
I heard the boy's footsteps as he paced up and down under our
window. In the morning everything returned to normal; the student went off to school and I decided I need not look in the
newspaper for a suicide report.

But to return to my sisters: it does not surprise me to find
Gizela appearing so seldom in my autobiography of those first ten
years, when Malvina was playing such a strong role. Gizela was
very kind to me—she couldn't ever be anything but kind—but
unlike Malvina she never let herself be inconvenienced by my
existence. Gizela was unquestionably my mother's favorite. She
resembled a citizen living in a despotically ruled country to whom
it never occurs to revolt because he is not bothered in his personal
life. When people met Gizela on the street, so pretty and so sweet,
they could never resist giving her a warm smile. I clearly remember that she was at one point the object of a deep, true, though
quite platonic love, which she did not reject but accepted with
her usual amiable expression.

The young man in question was the youngest of three brothers
in an eminent intellectual family with cultural achievements far
above the norm for Przemyśl. They were all lawyers—what else
could clever young Jews be in those days? The youngest of the
three hardly practiced his profession at all, and his brilliance
made him what I like to call a "genius without portfolio," after
a character in a novel by the Polish writer Przebyszewski. He was
similar to Gizela in temperament, with a benign disposition. He
must have been very unhappy when Gizela got engaged to a
young doctor. I was fourteen, and my instinct for espionage, so
typical of that age, helped me to see the situation clearly, but
without the tragic sympathy I had invested in Malvina's affairs.
The young man tactfully tried not to bother the engaged couple.
Only once did he show his true feelings. How well I remember
that evening when by chance Gizela, her fiancé Michael, and I

stopped by the delicatessen where the young lawyer usually ate his supper. He returned our friendly greetings, but then, obviously needing to share his feelings of resentment, he leaned over to me and whispered, *"Chamy miod pija a ty widziesz i nie grzemiesz Panie!"* ("The rabble drink mead, and thou, O God, seest and thunderest not!") [1]

Gizela's engagement was hard on me too, but in a more down-to-earth, even comical way. In those days no girl was ever left alone with a young man without her "elephant" or chaperone. This was especially enforced if the couple was engaged. Our parents were very strict in this regard, and after they had gone to bed I had to remain with the lovers as the "elephant." I took my role very seriously, but Gizela and Michael managed to persuade me to play watchman from the next room. They usually sat at the piano, she playing and he singing. I liked this arrangement: as soon as the music stopped and the whispering began, I could retreat into my own fantasies undisturbed.

I wonder if my presence actually helped Gizela to avoid any genuine sexual threat. As for me, the erotic excitement of the situation led to a kind of unconscious masturbation, common in adolescence, which was accompanied by a discharge. I immediately took advantage of the situation and turned to my future brother-in-law for help. He prescribed warm baths; I was gratified by his sympathy, and only my mother was disgruntled. Warm baths, according to her routine, should be allowed only on Fridays.

What a difference between my two sisters' weddings! I experienced Malvina's as something close to Greek tragedy, Gizela's as a charming Viennese operetta (light music was in fact played). The second wedding had less fanfare; Kasia was no longer with us, either. But I was given a lovely pink dress. I had a wonderful time.

This time I felt less deserted, for Gizela was to live right in

1. A quotation from a novel by Sienkiewicz, spoken by Zagłoba, a drunkard figure modeled after Falstaff.

Przemyśl, and I made frequent visits to her new home. Indeed she had to be contented with her little sister's company: she found out soon that childbearing seemed to be impossible for her. For seven years she remained one of those cases of sterility without any "organic" cause. Little was as yet known about psychology. Oddly enough, Gizela did become pregnant shortly after I left home and thus deprived her of a little sister.

I was overjoyed when her first child, Arthur (Tusio), was born. He was absolutely not, however, "old Rosenbach" stock, though he turned out to be very gifted artistically, not in music, as one might have expected, but in drawing. The youngster had, alas, a touch of the charlatan in him, reminding me of Jacek. For instance, as a joke he once ordered visiting cards with "Count" engraved on them and then quite seriously went about making mischief with them. Arthur's parents were overindulgent to this long-awaited child, and he grew up terribly spoiled.

Arthur died a gruesome death during the Nazi regime. For a long time I believed that his younger brother Leonard (Lonio) had also died, but recently I received a visit from his daughter Gay, my great-niece. Through her I learned with pleasure that Leonard and his family are living in England, where he is practicing medicine. My sister Gizela died in Australia, where her daughter Irene is still living.

As to Malvina's fate: she had four children, three of whom died before she did, one in early childhood. It was her first child, Ludwig, that she always loved best. In my childhood fantasies, I associated him with myself, reborn in the shape of a boy. At the same time I must have been extremely jealous of him. For a while, he was the only boy in the family (my brother being already grown up) and the center of everyone's love.

Ludwig had an unusually tragic end. Only eighteen when called to serve in World War I, he went through active combat at the front, was released at the end of the war in good health, and set out for home. Local tensions and aggressions were still aflame. Przemyśl, because of its strategic location, was at the center of the civil war between Poles and Ukrainians. Under Austrian domination these two groups had been fighting their own war for years, not always with weapons. World War I did not really unite them. Ukrainian and Polish boys together fought the enemies of the fatherland Austria, but inside the big war the small one continued.

Ludwig was marching home as a veteran, tired of fighting and expecting to go back to being a boy in late adolescence enjoying his mother's *piroszki* (filled pastries) and swimming in the San. This historic river divided the city into two parts, the west side Polish and the east side Ukrainian, a division that was not official but had gradually come about by itself. On the bridge Ludwig met a group of Ukrainian soldiers—I don't know whether he was alone or with his military unit. At any rate, while his family waited for him on the balcony of their house overlooking the beautiful San, he was wounded by a Ruthenian soldier. The wound was slight, but he developed the symptoms of tetanus and soon died.

Malvina reacted to the death of her most beloved child by lapsing into a psychotic state which I believe persisted until her own death. Going home only to sleep, she spent all her days at the grave of her son. The details of her psychosis and her death are not known to me. I know that the surviving brother and sister tried with their devotion to compensate for the loss of Ludwig, but to no avail. I still have in my possession a picture of that much-loved boy, taken some months before his death. There is something in the handsome, melancholy face that is prophetic of his early death.

I must speak here of a psychosomatic occurrence that seems extraordinary to me. Edward, the younger brother, did not resemble Ludwig in the least. Ludwig was dark, Edward blond; Ludwig was tall, Edward short, and so on. After his brother died, Edward tried in every possible way to be a substitute for his mother's favorite. Nature somehow came to his aid: he grew taller, his hair darkened, and eventually even his features and mannerisms bore a striking resemblance to those of his dead brother. (Even all this evidently did not cure Malvina's obsession.)

At a psychoanalytic meeting attended by Freud, I reported on this case. Freud was visibly skeptical, but I convinced him that my description was based on facts. In one sentence, he gave a beautiful explanation: "It is as if a tree were to claim all the sunlight for itself, leaving its companion behind in the shadow, without a chance to grow; but when the tree in front falls down, the one behind it will enjoy the sunbeams and thrive on them."

I have a vague impression that Edward later on became one of Hitler's victims. Ola, Malvina's daughter, survived, married, and taught in a Polish college. After her husband's death, she seemed to turn all her love toward me. The last letter I received from her ended with the words, "I am going to die today." My investigations with the Polish authorities confirmed that she died of tuberculosis on the day she wrote that letter. However from my recent contact with Leonard Oller I have learned that she is still alive, healthy, and active, and in frequent communication with the Ollers; she often provides her relatives with Polish delicacies, including the homemade rose-petal preserves I remember from my own Polish childhood. I am still unclear as to why I received the misinformation about her supposed death, and how the contact between us was broken.

IV

Mother

F I R S T let me confirm what the reader must already suspect: for most of my childhood and youth I hated my mother. And yet I do remember experiences suffused with positive feelings toward her. These occurred for the most part during the rare times when I was ill. She was the person I wanted to have by my bed when I had pains or fever; it was she who stayed with me when I had whooping cough, isolating herself from all her friends for fear of infecting them. She provided help and nursing care. She traveled to Lwów, the nearest large city, to buy pretty dresses for me, and more.

It was, unfortunately, also my mother who beat me—not to punish me, but as an outlet for her own pent-up aggressions. She let me feel the full force of the grudge she bore me for not being the boy she had wanted and expected. That is why it is painful for me to look back on that part of my childhood in which my mother played an important role.

It was not until I was in the prime of my own life as a woman and a mother that I learned what her childhood had been like and understood how hard it must have been. In the course of my autobiographical research I found out about the emotional deprivation she herself had suffered, and I now understand how isolated and lonely she must have felt. She was the daughter of Grandfather Leizor, whose repellent personality has already been mentioned, and of a woman who abandoned her family precipitously to run off with a lover. I wonder: could my mother's tyrannical vigil over the chastity of her daughters and her tendency to value status, conformity, and a good reputation above all else be the result of her mother's disgrace? My mother was an imposing individual and I believe that if she had grown up in a more secure emotional environment and had found definite personal goals and responsibilities, her ambition and willpower could have borne better fruit.

She was of course sent for one or two years to a boarding school in Switzerland, as Polish girls of good family usually were, but after that she went back into the destructive atmosphere of the Leizor home. I don't know when or how she met my father; probably it was through mutual friends. In any case it must have been a heady experience for this ambitious girl who valued "culture" but had had, so to speak, only a breath of it and therefore suffered from a quite natural sense of inferiority. Up to then, her aspirations had been large, but without aim. I would guess that the shocking experience of her own mother's defection, her intellectual insecurity, and an inner confusion of values were all reasons why her ambition as a mother centered around the good reputation of her daughters in the eyes of the world.

It is easy to see why I became the bane of her life. I was the rebellious one, storming ahead, completely free from any worry about my reputation. She had no sympathy for any of the tragic elements of my adolescence, caring only about the public image. She finally gave up her fight against my life goals when she was forced to realize her own powerlessness.

My mother ruled our model household like a despot, from a throne situated in a niche off the dining room. A huge brown

Dutch oven formed the back wall of this niche. She would stand leaning against this oven, supervising with a keen eye, or immersed in her own daydreams. It was from here that she handed down her commands to the cook or to the servant we called the *lokaj*, or butler. He would come into our bedrooms and the living room at five o'clock in the morning to light the giant ovens and to wax the floors, gliding around with foot-brushes strapped to his bare feet until the surfaces were mirror-smooth and gleaming. In the evenings he served us at supper, wearing a white glove on one hand—that is, if we had company. For everyday meals, my unofficial services were enough.

For years, mealtimes were a dreadful ordeal for me. My place was on my mother's left. Whenever something irritated her, causing a momentary outbreak of rage, she would give me a slap. My brother would often provoke me into giggling by making little noises and gestures. If my mother was in a bad mood, smack! a slap for Hala.

The arrangement of our apartment made meals even more of a hardship for me. The dining room and the kitchen were separated by three bedrooms, and every communication with the servants required a messenger: me, of course. "Bring the next course," or "The vegetables are not hot enough, take them back," meant "Hala, run!" I don't know which of us, the *lokaj* or I, suffered more under this tyranny.

I think with horror of those days, when servants were truly treated like slaves. We children were their friends and always took their side against my mother. There was a bond between us, which we often expressed by participating in their simple Catholic household rituals. There were many conspiratorial religious debates going on, the upshot always being that one should be a Catholic. I remember that on Sundays before my parents got up I was often taken along to early Mass. In one corner of the church was a painting of the Black Madonna of Czestochowa, the patroness of motherhood. I don't know why I venerated her especially. I bought a little picture of her, not knowing that she was supposed to be a helper in the various problems of motherhood, including those of unmarried mothers. This picture, painted by a Polish artist, still hangs in my house today. My whole childhood was filled with the pervasive spirit of Catholicism: I have already mentioned in an earlier chapter the funeral processions stimulating my childish thoughts about death and about my Jewish identity.

I never saw my mother working, only giving orders. She entered the kitchen only to have short talks with the cook, seldom picked up a sewing needle, and left every bit of work for others to do. She was a beneficiary of an economic system that exploited domestic help. It is interesting that when I was a child, work and tenderness were somehow interwoven in my associations. Perhaps this came from the misinterpreted observation that mothers of poor children spent more time caring for them than my mother spent with me, since she could afford servants and governesses. I suspect that despite my close relationship with Malvina, I longed for the love of my mother.

She more or less forbade us to go into the kitchen, declaring that cooks don't like to be disturbed in their work. Malvina had nevertheless somehow learned to bake superb tortes, but as for Gizela and me, we had no incentive to learn the art of cooking, and never did. Many of the household chores were carried out by the *lokaj* in a regular daily ritual; the other tasks were left to the female servants. For instance, there were countless oil lamps, and enormous crystal chandeliers in the salon and dining room, that had to be cleaned and filled and lit when it began to grow dark. As each lamp caught fire, the *lokaj* would say, "Blessed be Jesus Christ!" and we children would answer in chorus, "Forever and ever, amen!"

This evidently did not bother my mother. Her attitude toward religion was in a sense typical of her: she regarded it as just another social ceremony. Once a year, at New Year's, she appeared at the temple in her reserved box. But not to pray; there she would collect gossip about her daughters, to sustain her eternal preoccupation with "reputation." Those were never good days for me!

Another source of information about her daughters' reputations was the hairdresser, who came every day. As she arranged the elaborate chignons, she related to my mother the town gossip she had picked up since her last visit. Mostly it had to do with small scandals: the infidelities of married women and the lack of morality in girls from good families—even Jewish ones.

My mother had no influence on my education, and her contribution to my intellectual values only existed in a negative sense: I reacted against hers. My precocious love of "culture" came from my father and was therefore part German and part Polish in character. (Father's education had been in the German language, forced upon the Poles by political treaties.)

The prescribed schooling for girls ended at age fourteen, since the high schools were open to boys only. The public schools in Przemyśl were still imbued with the Austrian-German atmosphere, and children from the more cultured families received their education privately. Private schools were not coeducational. For girls there were two: the Hildschule and Miss Zofia Iwanicka's school. The former won historical importance through its serious attempts to improve the education of women. It was run by the two Hild sisters, who despite their respectability impressed one as being somehow grotesque. One was tall, the other short; they wore wigs and looked as if they had been cut out of a very old photograph. Most of their pupils were Jewish. For my morbidly ambitious mother, this was a signal to enroll her daughters elsewhere.

The other alternative was the private school of Miss Zofia Iwanicka, a furiously aggressive old maid. She took me under her wing, but only because I was a Rosenbach and intellectually promising. All my resentment of my mother was transferred to her. We did not have an idyllic time together when my parents took their trip to Switzerland (*en famille* but without me) and left me behind in Miss Iwanicka's charge.

It was a great relief to me when Miss Iwanicka retired and was replaced by a new headmistress, Mrs. Gawronska. Genuinely cultured, she was the wife of a well-known Polish patriotic writer. She was largely responsible for the upsurge of my Polish patriotism at the age of twelve, when I turned eagerly to Polish poetry and other Polish literature. This love for Polish poets has lasted all my life and always formed a bond with my country even after I left it for good, and even after its increasing anti-Semitism estranged me from Poland completely. My father also began to show an interest in Polish literature in his later life, but unfortunately it was just when his work began to demand all of his time.

My mother read mostly French books. She declared once, when I suggested that she read Władisław Reymont's *Chłopi (The Peasants)*,[1] "I read only books that concern *my* social class." My sisters were of course fascinated by Zola and Maupassant and read them in secret, or they read copies with certain pages sewed up by my mother to conceal the improprieties. I read whatever I wanted to read, and my mother had to resign herself.

The town of Przemyśl itself provided a goodly degree of cultural stimulation. I can say with some pride that in those days as well as later on certain centers of Jewish intelligentsia were often the main champions and carriers of the humanistic spirit in Poland. In Przemyśl the women of the Jewish upper middle class (wives of doctors, lawyers, etc.) read, shared, and disseminated international literature. They met in two literary clubs: the original "Czytelnia" ("The Reading Room") and its later offshoot "Ognisko" ("The Fireplace"). My mother was an active member of these societies, though not, I believe, a very popular one.

Nowadays when I meet people from Przemyśl, they invariably know something about the Rosenbach family. I notice that the image they have of my mother underscores her isolation; I too

1. It was for this novel that Reymont won the Nobel Prize for Literature in 1924.

always had the feeling that she was a lonely person. As they say, she did indeed interest herself in the affairs of the town, but not as a participant. She was, rather, a kind of well-wisher, what in high society is called a patroness. These people from Przemyśl speak with warmth and respect of my father and some of the other Rosenbachs: the girls were sweet and well-bred; the youngest was "crazy" but gifted—and she didn't end up in the gutter, as everyone had predicted, after all.

At the outbreak of World War I, when my parents fled to Vienna, they were able, with the fraction of their property they had salvaged, to maintain their former glory for some time. My husband and I succeeded in making their stay as comfortable as possible. This last phase of my relationship with my mother is a paradox wrought by time. Historical events actually made our relations warmer, and my professional skills helped me to care for her during her exile. My concern was deeply felt—for nothing can touch me as much as human suffering, especially that of the ones I love. My mother was able to accept with dignity and even a certain amount of humor the fact that my study of medicine, which she had so strenuously opposed, was proving to be a boon for the whole family.

As soon as we heard that my parents' house had not been destroyed in the war, they left Vienna for home. I said farewell to them in a mood not much different from what I had always felt when they left Vienna after a visit. We all took peace for granted: "This is the last war—mankind must have grown wiser through such suffering." But the prewar status quo was never restored. Ludwig was dead, our family's greatest sacrifice on the altar of the war beast; and it was *not* the end of all wars.

My father, as I have written, died soon after resuming his law practice, and Mother was left alone. When the Nazis invaded Poland in 1939, she went into hiding in the homes of various friends, often living in a basement. Here my memories fail; a veil has descended over these events. According to one version, the Nazis took nearly everything from my mother except for a few possessions; she was able to save her big diamond earrings. These earrings were treasured for far more than their monetary worth. In Jewish families they were a symbol of success and prosperity and were usually left to the oldest daughter. I am not very sure about what happened to them, though I have heard that they were requisitioned "legally" and "according to orders" by the Nazis. There still remained her very last possession, a little chest of gold-and-enamel demitasse spoons. This she left to me when she died a few years later in Przemyśl, in her own house. How do I know all this, I wonder, and what has become of the little chest? And why did my mother leave it to *me?* Did a sense of remorse touch her at the end?

For her daughters she made the normal process of identification with the mother very difficult. Only now do I realize fully how many of the positive ideals in my life are a reaction against her. Yet in my heart I have kept to this day a yearning for her love.

V

Relatives

WHAT A DIFFERENCE there was between my mother's and my father's people! Though apparently from more or less the same milieu, they could not have stood farther apart in spirit. Their social, cultural, and emotional attitudes were diametrically opposed. All they had in common was their Jewishness and their ability to endure the hardships that came with it.

My mother's family did not belong to the class of really wealthy Jews. For the most part they were well-to-do, and their life goal was to be rich. Their motto was "Money will buy anything," even social prestige, which was of paramount importance to my mother's generation because it represented a way out of the ghetto.

I was born relatively late in my parents' marriage, after my mother had become quite assimilated into my father's social status, which was higher than hers when they first met. This is not to say that she avoided her own relatives, merely that we had more contact with my father's side of the family. One of the reasons may have been the separation of her parents, which occurred before I was born. In our sheltered lives, we as children learned about it only through hearsay, years later.

My mother's parents had owned a fabric shop. It was managed entirely by my grandmother and a young male clerk; my grandfather took little part in the business. It was not the sort of situation, however, that one sees in some orthodox Jewish families where the wife works to support the family and the husband spends all his time praying. No, my grandfather Leizor was not pious. He sat all day in the store as a sort of masculine figurehead, while the other two ran the business.

The marriage was not a happy one. One day my grandmother left for Vienna, taking with her the handsome clerk and all the money. There she opened a fabric shop of her own with money she had been hoarding for years without her husband's knowledge. She then obtained a divorce from my grandfather and married the young clerk.

I remember visiting them in Vienna. There were two children from this second marriage: a very beautiful daughter who later married a pedantic businessman (there is a memory of bedspreads in their house looking as smooth and white as ice); and a son, Lolo, who was about four years older than I, the writer of the suicide note mentioned in an earlier chapter. Grandmother Fass's house in Vienna seems to have left only one other impression on my child's mind: it was overrun with vermin. (Vienna was known to be a bug-infested city.) Later on, we used to stay at an elegant Viennese hotel.

My grandmother's story probably sounds prosaic, but I have always sensed a romantic tone in it. In those days such a step was an act of social revolution.

She had had four children by her marriage to Leizor. Beside my mother, there were "lovely Aunt Helena," Uncle Willy, and Uncle Bernard. My mother must have had a good relationship with her siblings. Aunt Helena, the youngest in the family, seems to have been in the same relation to my mother as I was to Malvina. She was very beautiful, but, as I remember from later years, not very clever or intellectually gifted. She married a judge; her three daughters remained my closest friends even after they moved to nearby Stryj where I spent summers with them. These three cousins were later killed by the Nazis.

Uncle Willy and Uncle Bernard must have left Przemyśl at a fairly early age to live with their mother in Vienna. Occasionally they came to visit us. They had forgotten nearly all the Polish they had known. Both of them were well-educated and were engineers, a very unusual profession for Jews in those days, the only choice, normally, being medicine or law. My uncles were extremely assimilated; they spoke the Viennese dialect and did not impress one as being Jewish.

When I knew Grandfather Leizor, he lived alone in Przemyśl. Regarded by all of us as a *quantité négligeable,* he nonetheless had an unwritten veto power in the life of the family. As we have seen, Malvina's happiness was sacrificed to his stringent orthodoxy. Nobody liked old Leizor, and I, the youngest in the clan, could see through his character with the intuition of an unusually sensitive child. He had a habit of coming over on Sunday mornings and presenting each of us children with a four-*groschen* piece. I would hurl the coin away from me every time and run from him.

He limped and supported himself with a thick cane, with which he was always threatening to hit us children. But what I most hated about him was the meanness of character betrayed by his hairstyle and clothes. It was obvious that he wished to look like a "modern" Jew, trying just like many others to appear to be of the "intelligentsia." Therefore, though he didn't shave off his sideburns (*peyes*), he cut them so short that they were scarcely visible. His coat was not the regular *Bekesche* of orthodox Jews, but rather a longish frock coat. He was taking no chances with God; he was, of course, a "modern" Jew, but you never can tell—one day he might have to stand up and be judged by the God of the Talmud and he would be able to say, "But I wore *peyes* and a long coat!"

I was very young, but I hated that limping grandfather for his hypocrisy, and I think that my character, while it was influenced by my father's high-minded spirit, also owes a lot to the negative influence of my grandfather—my desire not to be like *him!* I know several highly esteemed men whom I dislike for no apparent reason. In most cases there is something of Grandfather Leizor in them that I instinctively sense.

My mother tried to maintain a certain kind of loyalty to both of her parents. She accepted Leizor's Sunday visits, but also visited her runaway mother and her new family during our summer excursions to Austrian resorts via Vienna. Lolo's visits to Przemyśl were further proof of my parents' impartiality.

Grandmother Fass had sisters who were much more interesting than she. Whereas she was a liberated woman only as far as her erotic life was concerned, her sisters were true eccentrics, such as may appear in every culture under different guises. One of them, Aunt Leika, was quite rich—people estimated that she was worth millions—but she never stopped whining about the financial straits that were reducing her to penury. This was her standard topic of conversation. When she met Malvina's fiancé for the first time, in our house, she told him about her "poverty" and held her hand out, obviously expecting a donation. He was troubled and concerned that we should leave the "poor lady" in such want! She was a well-known moneylender and held in her hands the fate of more than one debt-laden aristocratic family. The old woman murdered by Raskolnikov in *Crime and Punishment* is the very image of Leika. She was an eccentric personally, but in her profession a familiar figure in our society—and its cancer.

I remember that one day my father came home furious. He and some colleagues, lawyers and judges, had gone to a delicatessen to have their usual bite to eat at lunchtime. Leika suddenly appeared out of nowhere (she spied on the comings and goings of her creditors) and sprang over to the cashier's table where Count X was just in the act of changing a thousand-crown note. She grabbed the note and handed him back two hundred crowns, hissing in her Polish-Jewish dialect, "Is this your bill? You owe me eight hundred crowns, including interest. There's your change, two hundred crowns."

This incident is still remarkably clear to me, probably because it is part and parcel of my deep, innate refusal to identify in any way with my mother's clan. Their personalities were a constant reminder of how *not* to be. This is rational in itself, but it is also an indirect rejection of my mother.

"Holy Malvina" who, when I was a child, gave all she could to the poor, would have had difficulty in recognizing that she and stingy Aunt Leika had something in common. Leika indulged herself in her unwillingness to give; Malvina overcompensated for her unwillingness by wanting to give everything away. But they shared a compulsive cleanliness. Leika seemed to be trying to whitewash her dirty business practices by maintaining an immaculate outward appearance. Even her silk wig gleamed with constant washing. (In her orthodox society, the women had to shave off their hair and wear scarves on their heads.) Malvina used to wash her hands obsessively to get rid of her neurotic horror of dirt. But I hope that the similarity between certain neurotic traits of Malvina and those of Leika does not obscure the fundamental differences between these two women. Malvina was one of the noblest people I ever knew, Leika one of the meanest.

Another of Grandmother Fass's sisters, Aunt R.F., was a woman far ahead of her time and even more eccentric than Leika. A gorgeous apparition, elegantly and fashionably groomed, she was never without a cigar in her mouth. She associated with distinguished men (not with their wives) and included learned rabbis among her friends, though herself an agnostic. I heard that she was a noted authority on Schopenhauer and was often consulted by other scholars for elucidations, sources, etc. She was not looking either for recognition or for status; she was simply interested in Schopenhauer. In later generations there have been, and still are, many women interested in philosophy; they can be found in the graduate schools, or, equipped with Ph.D.s, they fill posts as professors, librarians, and so forth. Many of them nowadays are active in the women's liberation movement. Aunt R., however, was not "modern" in that sense. She was really more of a unique character than a type. External, worldly advances meant nothing to her, nor did her lack of formal schooling or official degrees.

Aunt R.'s "bad reputation" made it not quite proper for young girls from good families to associate with her. She was considered sexually disreputable; it was said that her husband had left her because she behaved like a man and not like a decent woman. I know exactly what this meant because I had the information directly from her: enjoyment of the sexual act was then considered to be for men only; women were designed by nature merely to be passive objects of their sex partners' drives. Aunt R. protested actively against this concept and according to local gossip even encouraged her three daughters to practice free love. Over the years I came to realize that Aunt R. was a genuine pioneer. Though she never demonstrated for women's equality and never took the suffragettes of her day seriously, yet she served the cause of woman's liberation manifestly and consistently by her whole way of life.

It was during my friendship with her that I learned that respectable women of her generation normally were frigid. I thought of her many years after her death, when as chairman of a roundtable meeting I led a discussion on frigidity. What an innovator she was, without portfolio, without roundtable!

The aunt who had the most influence on my young life and the person who took over my upbringing and my affections after Malvina married was Aunt Frania. She belonged to my father's family, which brings us, as I have indicated, into a totally different atmosphere. My father's relations were far less well-off but culturally much more assimilated than my mother's. They had modified their Jewish traditions with new values; and money, the idol of my mother's family, was considered merely one of life's necessities.

My father's immediate family included Uncle Leon, Uncle Bernard, Aunt Frania, Aunt Sonja, and my Grandmother Rosenbach. The two uncles seem to have been fairly banal individuals. Uncle Leon was a photographer. I cannot remember that he and his own family played any part in my life. Uncle Bernard was a figure of fun for us as children. I don't know what he did for a living; I only know that he clearly suffered from a chronic depression that may have been the cause of his perpetual idleness. Whenever one of us met him and asked him where he was going, he would give the same answer. "To have a cup of coffee." Something is probably missing from this washed-out portrait in my memory. At any rate, it was obviously my father who had the desire, force, and brains to add glory to the name Rosenbach.

According to family history, the name Rosenbach itself connotes respectability and financial stability. The Jews who immigrated into Poland in the reign of Casimir the Great were assigned family names according to the amount of gold they could pay for them. The less common the chosen name was, the more it cost. King Casimir had invited this wave of immigration not out of any love for the Jews, who were at this point in history homeless and shunted from pillar to post, but as part of a shrewd plan. Poland was just beginning to develop industries and expand its trade with foreign nations, and it needed a group with experience in commerce. As such, the Jews were permitted to immigrate, and the results were entirely satisfactory. The history of the Jews included many such migrations into and out of countries, with and without bloody persecutions. The most recent ones took place in my native country, Poland, within my own lifetime.

My mother complained at every opportunity that my father was using her dowry to support his own relatives. This may have been partly true, perhaps in the case of my father's mother. But our old, sweet *Babcia* ("granny") Rosenbach was the sunshine in my and my sisters' lives. From our grandiose apartment on the second floor we would run—especially me—downstairs to the poor, two-room apartment of *Babcia* and her two daughters Sonja and Frania. There we learned about *belonging* in the warmest sense of the word. Here past images begin to merge and blur; I am not quite sure which emotional memory belongs to *Babcia* and which to Aunt Frania. I only know that not too long ago I received a letter forwarded to me by a young relative in Israel, written in a clear hand and full of the same characteristic human warmth that emanated from both *Babcia* and Aunt Frania.

After Malvina's marriage left me feeling abandoned and alone, it was natural that I should turn to some member of my father's family—natural that it was my father's sister and mother who filled my emotional vacuum. Aunt Frania became my close companion as well as a strong influence on my education. The image comes back to me of her lovely small figure clad in a lavender blouse with a black velvet collar and buttons; in this recurring image in my mind she is always smiling, always a friend.

Out of necessity both my aunts had to hold jobs. Aunt Sonja worked for the city government and Aunt Frania was a teacher who, according to popular reports, showed great pedagogical talent in guiding the children in her care. Neither aunt gave up her job after getting married. Aunt Sonja, however, had a great many troubles that absorbed her, and unfortunately lost both her husband and her two children. After that I never saw her when she wasn't on the verge of tears. Aunt Frania remained unmarried long enough after Malvina's marriage to become an enormous influence on me during the "latency" period, approximately the years from eight to eleven.

Aunt Frania felt that I was intellectually precocious, and also that I had potential literary talent. My written schoolwork was actually never outstanding; nonetheless I had always wanted to be a writer, even when I was very young. This desire was not based on any confidence that I was a creative poet or full of an abundance of ideas waiting to be written down. It was instead a conviction: "I shall be a writer, but first I have to learn a lot to have something to write about." And I did show signs of a definite literary aptitude in my childhood, not in my school assignments, but in the poetry I wrote at home and little plays that were put on in a children's theater in Przemyśl. The plays were really my work, though it was popularly thought that Aunt Frania had written them. Cases like this show very clearly that a child's talent, existing as a tiny bud, needs an external stimulus, needs watering and sun, if it is ever going to blossom.

Aunt Frania's intellectual interests later led her into the literary circles of the Polish intelligentsia. She married a prosperous photographer and had three children. She had one lively daughter, Paula, who married the son of a famous Polish writer; she and her husband, who owns a Polish bookstore and has edited a Polish encyclopedia, now play a distinguished role in Polish cultural life in Paris. I remember the noisy and vigorous fights Aunt Frania's sons Emil and Stach would have with each other when they were children. Whenever they were expected to pay a visit, my mother went around the apartment trying to hide everything breakable. People said that Aunt Frania wasn't bringing them up properly. But I believe that her intuition was leading her in the right direction. The way she handled her wild boys is sanctioned by modern child psychology; she allowed them to find, without outside interference, the outlets they needed for their natural aggressions. At any rate these "wild" ones grew up into well-adjusted and successful men in spite of the destructive influence of the gradual deterioration of their parents' marriage. "The Photographer," as we called him, developed in later years a severe mental disturbance of a paranoid nature which disrupted their family life. I don't know any further details. But Aunt Frania lives in my memory as a truly benevolent power in my young life.

I knew Grandfather Rosenbach only from his portrait, which hung on the wall in my father's study. (Only now does it occur to me that his portrait, like my father's family, was excluded from my mother's domain.) The construction of this painting fascinated me. It was one of those old-fashioned portraits made up of many pieces of wood glued together, so that different aspects of it would come into view according to one's angle of vision. I remember very distinctly the fine features of my grandfather. It was the face of a thinker, and bore not the slightest resemblance to the bearded ancestors on my mother's side. I believe that he died before I was born. I never knew what his profession was, only that he left his widow and five children in very precarious financial circumstances.

VI

Early Adolescence

EVEN BEFORE my period of political activism, I had begun a vigorous adolescent rebellion against my parents. I had graduated from Mrs. Gawronska's school at age fourteen, and now was expected to live the idle life of a debutante under my mother's tutelage until I married. I refused to accept such an existence. I started to write, and with my first article in the local paper I received full recognition and a steady job as a weekly columnist. I had been declared a "great talent," and I believe I had one. But at the same time I was too serious and realistic to accept this talent as a solid foundation for my freedom. I wanted to go away and to learn. I was to reach this goal eventually, but meanwhile there were harsh realities in the way.

Even my father opposed me in my battles at home. It was hard for him to acknowledge that a full-fledged feminine creature could have talents and interests his society ascribed only to boys. Woman's role in society was supposed to be a passive one. Though he had never tried to deny my female identity, he began to fear my "craziness."

Often a small, seemingly trivial incident will change one's fate. At some moment during that period I met a young man— small, unimpressive, even dull, but obsessed with ambition. A law student, he had set his sights uncompromisingly on becoming a Professor of Jurisprudence. (He later reached his goal.) We took long walks together and he described to me the intellectual life at the University of Kraków, while I complained about the growing dreariness and frustration of my life in Przemyśl. And it was this young Mr. Taubenschlag, the last person I would have expected it from, who helped me open the door of my prison: "Well," he said, "take your college entrance exam and leave home!"

I knew that the certificate one received after passing this examination, called the *Abitur,* was an "open sesame" admitting its bearer to almost any European university. But it seemed impossible for me to pass it. My schooling, as I have described, had been very limited, and my immediate environment (that is, my mother) was extremely discouraging. I began my war against these obstacles. To an adolescent, the first step seemed obvious. I had to get away from home!

This project was twice carried through. The first time it had the look of a childish comedy. I had no plan, no accomplice, hardly any money. My revolutionary gesture must have looked like the result of reading too many detective stories (which I never read): I went down to the railroad station and, to confuse my pursuers, bought two tickets in opposite directions. What I remember most clearly is the trip itself: I wept as if my heart were broken, imagining how my poor father would come home that evening and find his darling Hala gone. I mourned with him for his loss. I've forgotten how I got home, but not the depression that followed. I felt vanquished.

Yet my hope of one day gaining my *Abitur* was sustained by my sense of community with other young people. Several young men offered to help me with lessons, but unfortunately these attempts ended in small love tragedies. To convince my parents that I was in earnest, I left home once again. This drama was more rationally planned, and I returned only on the condition that my father sign a written contract binding him to help me attain my *Abitur* in every way he could, including the hiring of teachers. My insistence on a written guarantee meant, implicitly, that I didn't trust him not to retract a spoken promise under the influence of my mother. He never did free himself from that influence and in spite of the contract our conflict could never be truly resolved, as he sensed that my craving to go to college was tied up with a deep-seated desire for freedom.

Even after the contract was signed, I remained restless and impatient and made all kinds of sporadic efforts to speed up my progress. I spent a couple of months in a private school for girls in Lwów and came back, without the *Abitur*. I also spent half a year in Zürich studying sociology under Professor Grünberg.

In Zürich I came into contact with a colony of Russian students, most of them political fugitives from Czarism. They had settled along the Dolderstrasse, making this residential district notoriously noisy for their bourgeois neighbors. They gathered together to engage in continuous loud discussions on the theory of revolution. I remember that their great intellectual leader was Plekhanov. They would discuss for hours the problems of quantity and quality in systems of economics. I sat there burning with the desire to learn how to make a revolution, but I heard only windy explications of economic theories.

The most revered person in this group was Vera Figner, the Russian woman physician and revolutionist, who had come to Switzerland after serving twenty-two years in the Schlüsselburg Fortress for assassinating one of the tyrannical Czarist governors. (Her own father was a general in the Russian army.) She came out of prison planning new deeds in the cause of the Revolution. In the meantime she indulged in theorizing, like the others.[1]

I returned home unsatisfied. I hadn't understood the students' language or ideas very well, and at the same time I found them

1. She told the story of her revolutionary career in her widely read book *Memoirs of a Revolutionist* (New York: International Publishers, 1927).

personally too fanatical and too removed from reality. Yet I had actually learned a great deal in that short time, and I had caught something of their idealism, their thirst for social and political freedom.

It took me about five years of preparation to win my *Abitur*. During that time I went through a personal transformation in which love and politics were intertwined.

In that era before the First World War Poland was a whirlpool of clashing social currents. In my immediate environment, conflicting ideologies had been transmitted through three generations of ancestors who had borne the stigma of being Polish Jews. Even when one left the ghetto it took a long time to cast off the effects of this invisible mark. Although there were striking differences between the cultural levels of the older and the younger generations, the "generation gap" was minimal compared to today. In some families, religious orthodoxy extended over several generations, though in others a grandfather would still be deeply rooted in orthodoxy and the grandson assimilated to the point of complete identification with the Poles. The assimilated young people took an active part in Polish political demonstrations, festivals, etc., and there were even some who joined in the short-lived outbreaks of revolt against the Austrian Empire.

The Zionist movement had not yet developed a wide following when I was young. Politically active Jews, when not involved in assimilation through Polish patriotism, or when frightened by the ever-lurking Polish anti-Semitism, turned toward the Polish socialist movement. (This is not to say that the socialist movement was free of anti-Semitic tendencies. But these came later.)

In general the Poles in Galicia in the time of my youth were intensely patriotic. They mourned for their lost fatherland and the famous phrase *"Jeszcze Polska nie zginęła"* ("Poland is still undefeated") had a real, very serious meaning. When the Austrian government became more democratic and the Poles were granted increased representation in the Parliament, they moved further toward an open political battle for nationhood. However, the group of Polish delegates to Parliament was itself split by internal disputes.

My generation's interest in socialism and in the worker's movement was sparked by news of the social revolution spreading through Russia, especially by its romantic aspects—the danger, the heroic self-sacrifice. There were of course other elements in socialism that were devoid of the revolutionary spirit and limited to party politics and short-term improvement of the workers' lot. This was not the form of socialism to which I, during my prolonged adolescence, subscribed. Let me add that revolutionism can never be defined simply through its social application; it is an attribute of individuals who are drawn to everything that is newly formed, newly won, newly achieved.

It was entirely consistent with my personality to become active in the socialist movement, especially in teaching and organizational work, when I was still in my teens. I had learned of the exploitation of the peasants as a little girl in my father's carriage; and I hated my mother's bourgeois materialism. My close friends all supported the Socialist Party; so did I, though I never became an official member. But 1905, the year of the first general elections in Galicia, found me in the ranks of activist youth, participating in a typically adolescent-revolutionary way.

I can't say that we represented the views of Przemyśl youth in general—there were very few of us then. Even later on in Vienna, when there were more of us, we did not function independently but appeared at gatherings under the aegis of an adult political group, the Socialist Workers. I remember that as a student at the University of Vienna I tried with some friends to join the Polish Workers' Party. We were thrown out bodily. They did not want our help.

In Przemyśl I suffered the inevitable youthful disillusionment over the integrity of politicians, in connection with the actions of a local labor leader. Up to that time, I had considered every worker a builder for the future, every socialist leader a hero, and had been ready to submit my own personality to their superior strength and wisdom. The realization of this particular labor leader's inferior ethical standards was a traumatic experience.

This did not discourage me, however, from further political activity. I became a sensation in my native town, since my father was a socially prominent person. He was a liberal, but certainly not a Social Democrat, and my political development set me in open opposition to him. Yet in spite of our political differences he tried not to let me down; he remained loving and was ready for a long time to defend me when I was ostracized by bourgeois society.

A scene from this period of my naïve political revolt comes back to me. The mounted police had blockaded our group of radical demonstrators. Eager for heroic deeds, I threw myself in front of the horses. The police arrested me and notified my father, asking him what they should do with me. "Lock her up," was his verdict, which of course was not carried out, to my extreme annoyance. My father was a very wise man.

Yet although my mind was ready to surrender to socialist ideals, my self-esteem needed something more. The "old Rosenbach" quality had stayed with me, in the form of a narcissistic ego-ideal not easy to gratify in the humble role of a party soldier. I had to find some further outlet. Also there was constant pressure within me to leave home—at least emotionally, since it could not at first be rationally accomplished physically. My hate of my mother and horror of identification with her, my dangerous love for my father and the difficulties of identifying with him, and my separation from Malvina—all these problems could be resolved in only one way: I needed a stronger relationship with a person outside my family yet endowed with qualities that would make a transition from my father-identification possible.

In truth, behind all my political enthusiasm there was just such a person. I have seldom seen so pure an Oedipal situation as was this fusion of love and politics. L. was married and sixteen years older than I, yet for many years, until I met Felix Deutsch, he remained the center of my femininity.

The emotional situation with him was similar to my relationship with my father. For L. also, I was the prettiest and smartest girl, the one with the "big eyes" he loved so much. I was L.'s daughter and his son in one person! I became the best lieutenant in his political "army." Our love was full of passion, happiness, tragedy. In the unwritten annals of Przemyśl, it is the *chronique scandaleuse* of a girl from a good family.

My mother raged. My father understood. "When you think it over," he said, "what other man could she fall in love with in this dull town?" For L. was not only a political and revolutionary leader. He was a man of good education, he had been all over the globe, he was well-read, and above all he was forceful—passionate in his loves and hates.

The following memories have remained unusually clear; their emotional intensity made them unforgettable. Of course they are not fully objective, and the places of events have sometimes been blotted out, or transferred from Przemyśl to Vienna and vice versa. Sometimes only the emotional atmosphere has been retained and the forgotten actual situation has had to be reconstructed. This may have led to some errors . . . but it often is the only way to bring back the past.

The scene in Przemyśl which we were later to call our "engagement" lives in me still, as clear as yesterday. It was a political rally in the open air. Instead of a political speech, the crowd found itself listening to an indirect but glowing declaration of love. L. confessed, in front of the gathering, to a recent abatement of idealistic striving, but added, "there come moments of renewal . . . ," referring to his love for me.

This happened just after my sixteenth birthday, in the period just before I decided to study for the *Abitur*. I was seeking to fill up the emptiness of my life through my writing and through private lessons in art history given by a teacher from the local high school. (Art history was considered a very "modern" subject for a young girl to be studying.) I had known L. at first primarily as a public figure. He had assumed the leadership of the Social

Democratic Party in Przemyśl and brought together the disparate workers' organizations under one banner. The Social Democrats had unquestionably brought about a great improvement in the workers' situation in Przemyśl: for example, the whole system of old-age and health insurance for workers now became a vital concern. L. was already an important figure in the international socialist movement.

But I also knew L. through my family. He had been a close friend of my sister Gizela's husband, Michael Oller, ever since their student days at the University of Kraków. My brother-in-law was not politically active but was connected with the working class through his work as a doctor in the workmen's medical insurance program. L. was a frequent guest at Gizela's house. He would often tease me, especially about my artistic enthusiasms. Then we had no premonition of how very soon his cool, benevolent interest in me would turn into passion.

The erotic character of our relationship, ever growing in intensity, could not remain hidden for long. The strong love that bound us together for many years had undertones of tragedy from the very beginning, but suffering hid itself behind political activity and gratifying service in the socialist cause. At first our love had an underground existence, and our meetings, outside our party activities, were limited to walks on the *Schlossberg*— romantic walks, golden with the light from a setting sun and full of suppressed passion. I was fascinated by the split in L.'s personality between the practical, energetic leader of his party and the sentimental, emotional lover of a very naïve adolescent girl, whose love he awakened in spite of himself.

During this period when our love was so to speak homeless, we talked not only about his past and future ambitions in behalf of his (and my) ideology but also of his fantasies. This realistic political leader, who submitted himself to the rules of his party even when he couldn't identify with them, was at heart a dreamer. I was perhaps the only one who knew that in his most intimate fantasies he was, like Christ, taking upon himself the cross of suffering in order to save mankind from its misery. He was not a man of religious belief, but his dedication to his humanitarian goals had an element of ecstasy surpassing the attitude of a mere political leader.

The genesis of L.'s revolutionary spirit had a typically adolescent character, but it matured with him and led him to great achievements. His father was a reactionary capitalist, though not extremely wealthy; his mother was a quiet woman tyrannized by her husband and seems to have been very attached to L., her oldest son. The revolutionary orientation of L.'s political activity can already be seen fully formed in his early family life.

The metamorphosis from personal motivation into an ideology did not begin, I believe, until his student years in Kraków, where he was deeply impressed by socialism and joined the youth movement. In Polish high schools and universities, the students were strongly influenced by events in Russia and inspired to fight for the ideals of the French Revolution. Sociological change had also called into being a new proletariat in Poland: the class-conscious workers whose increasing poverty became the strongest propaganda against social injustice. In those years Polish students were so involved in social causes that it was generally considered obligatory to treat purely cultural pursuits as a luxury and to avoid them.

In high school, L. made himself financially independent of his father by typing and selling little pamphlets containing plot synopses and explications of the German classics that were required reading in the schools. The students found them a blessing and bought them enthusiastically. I looked down on this enterprise of his youth. I argued that they kept their readers from reading and thinking on their own, and jokingly called him a corrupter of young minds. When I looked at these pamphlets years later, I was impressed by his grasp of the psychological implications in the works he summarized.

Later on I had the opportunity to point out to him, again jokingly, that I was providing him with a similar shortcut to culture, when his work in Parliament and the preparation of speeches left him no time to read books outside his professional sphere. It was the same with art and music: I often made him come with me to museums, exhibitions, and Vienna's great concerts, acting as his guide and interpreter.

L.'s speeches were masterpieces. He was a true orator, though by no means a demagogue. He was able to inflame his audiences and incite them to perform revolutionary deeds by the sincerity and intense passion of his own convictions. In his speeches he was extremely aggressive against political opponents, but his attacks were seldom personal, and he never misrepresented the actual facts. Above all, his oratory convinced one that he himself was genuinely ready to make every sacrifice for his beliefs. I was eager to share this mission with him. I longed to suffer and sacrifice with him for mankind, for the suffering proletariat.

By and by our outdoor meetings on the *Schlossberg* ceased to be satisfying: there was no protection from the weather or from curious onlookers. Meanwhile I had begun to study for my college entrance examination and in the evenings was using the room in my father's office where the clerks worked during the day. It had proved to be a good refuge where I could study in peace, and now it also became the haven for our brief rendezvous. L. would first check to see if I was there, with the help of the caretaker, Mr. Horak, who used to let him into the house after the gate was closed for the night. We would content ourselves with one embrace and L. would go back home to his family after a long solitary walk along the San. I suffered a great deal from the ever-present awareness that he was married, although I was sure he did not love his wife.

He was supposed by the town gossips to be a "ladies' man." I never knew the origin of these rumors—perhaps the occasional brief affairs he had had as a young man. I heard L.'s supposed infidelities talked about on all sides, but as far as I can remember they didn't interfere with my feelings. For my own image of L. was that of an ideal revolutionary hero. Our erotic relationship never changed that image and for me he always remained that hero. And the fact that, as far as I know, he had ceased to love his wife even before he met me, unburdened at least part of my guilt feelings.

Of course there were many elements in his actual character that nourished the hero image in me. He had two missions in life: he saw his identity divided between the pragmatic leader of a political party and the revolutionary waiting for the right moment for action. The second mission formed the strongest bond between us; I had a deep conviction that he was indeed a true revolutionary. As I think of him now, many years later, and in the light of the present, I still feel that he was one of those few men who are able, in Freud's phrase, to "disturb the world's slumber."

He had some values that were not revolutionary and that he shared with a conservative society. Within the framework of socialism he worked for progressive goals. But to have it openly known that he was having an affair with a middle-class girl from a good family—no. That would discredit the socialist movement as well as its leader. Such behavior in a mature man and a member of a solid middle-class profession (he was a lawyer) would arouse the animosity of all respectable citizens. And it is true that in this period even the progressive socialist worker retained his conservative outlook on domestic matters and looked very critically on overt marital infidelity. L., as I gradually realized but at the same time denied, had a double standard: he was liberal on sexual matters, as the spirit of the times and of his politics would lead one to expect, but he was outwardly a moral conservative who conformed officially to the requirements of his bourgeois milieu and wished to keep our relationship a secret.

It could be that his preservation of a sham marriage was a concession to his wife and children rather than to society. Perhaps a neurotic attachment to his wife also played a part. I told myself that I didn't care. This was untrue, for though I wasn't jealous I heartily detested the whole secretive ambiance. This was a topic we seldom talked about, by a kind of tacit agreement.

I know now that my own psychic dependency, rooted in an Oedipal childhood, bound me to just this sort of relationship, and that I myself was responsible for his failure to make a positive move. Many years after we parted, when life once again brought us together in a short encounter, he reproached me that by my absolutely undemanding submission to him I had precluded any attempt on his part to get a divorce. Here again autobiography has given me a chance to reevaluate events by reliving them. My relationship with L. seems to me now an exact duplicate of my earlier relationship to my parents and a classic example of an Oedipal situation: the man much older than I; the older, unloved wife; and the impossibility of dissolving their marriage. I could not marry my father; I could not marry L. And therefore I sustained the ambivalent situation, in effect a stalemate, frustrated my own desire for happiness, and nourished L.'s fantasies of self-sacrifice.

During his absences, and when I was dissatisfied with my own work, I would begin to feel estranged from him. I loved him intensely and could never entirely abandon my faith in him, but I was seldom totally free of doubts. Many times I tried to break off the relationship, but his despair would have such a strong effect on me that I could never go through with it. I wanted to be his fellow soldier in the struggle for the goals we held in common. And yet I also wanted my rights as a woman. I wanted, I thought, to be his wife! Ambiguity and frustrated desire drove me into the refuge of continual political activity.

Though I constantly resisted L.'s argument that it is not knowledge or theories but *results* that count in the service of the revolution, I did tend more and more toward direct work with the people. I headed discussion groups, which the organized workers badly needed. Though I was young and in a state of emotional turmoil, my approach to reality was quite mature. I not only marched and sang the *Marseillaise*, I also turned out to be a good organizer, and brought into being the first organization of working women in Przemyśl, at a time when there were very few of them anywhere. Unfortunately my good intentions were accompanied by a complete lack of experience and limited understanding of social forces.

In the workers' struggle against exploitation, the women generally didn't play an active role as yet. The men wanted to improve their lot so that their women wouldn't have to go out to work and neglect their home obligations. Working-class women were generally satisfied to give their men passive support and hope that necessity would not drive them out of their homes to work.

Of course this state of affairs did not appeal to me in the least! And I exploited the working women's attachment to me to persuade them to undertake an incredibly ill-timed strike, at a time of year when there was no market for the men's shirts they made at their factory. I didn't know that a strike can be effective only under certain conditions, and I thought that the workers' determination and solidarity were the only decisive factors: *"Alle Räder stehen still wenn dein starker Arm es will."* ("All the machines will stop, if only your strong arm wills it.") I was also proud of the fact that I was the organizer of the first strike by women in our town.

Amazingly, despite the predictable fiasco, the women stayed behind me. If it had been merely a question of enthusiasm and solidarity, the strike could have been called a success. We used the time not spent picketing, etc., to discuss social and cultural problems. The women themselves chose the topics, and I had to reread books I had only skimmed before to be able to discuss them with the group. It was a happy time for me. I was learning how much potential talent and craving for knowledge lay hidden behind those work-worn faces.

Thus L. and I spent several years in the happiness of working together and the misery of continual partings. I was not ready to give up my relationship with him. In 1907, destiny came to our aid. L.'s election as a delegate to Parliament transferred a large part of his political life to Vienna, and my ambition to study at a university gave me a good reason for leaving Poland.

VII

Vienna

A T L O N G L A S T the big day had come: I was ready to take the university entrance examination. For "private" candidates (those who were not attending a regular high school) it was given in two places, Lwów and Kraków, both for men only. I had to get special permission to take it. (Not long afterward, women were granted the right to take this examination on the same terms as men; it was a giant step forward in their emancipation.) In February 1907 I passed the examination and the world stood open before me.

I now hesitated about my choice of profession. I wanted to be a writer, but I also wanted, because of my identification with my father, to study law. The first goal was somehow obscure for me, the second closed by reality. The law schools were not yet open to women. When I later successfully petitioned with two other suffragettes to open the University of Vienna law school to women, it was for the sake of general principles, and no longer for personal aims.

Probably it was my social ideology that made me matriculate

at the University of Vienna School of Medicine. I admired Käthe Kollwitz [1] and planned to be a pediatrician like her. I must admit that my heart was not wholly in my studies and that my victory in the battle for college soon came to be used as a means toward furthering other aims, such as my love relationship, intertwined with political activism. The important thing, however, is that my ambition to study medicine was never given up.

This purposeful study undoubtedly helped me to strengthen my identity, and my love for L. had a stabilizing influence. Still, I was very much an adolescent during this period. With all my idealism, sincere impulse to be free, and revolutionary fervor, there was a strong narcissistic bent to all my activities. It had been nurtured in my childhood (the girl with the beautiful eyes, etc.) and reinforced by the personal frustrations of adolescence. Usually a girl's adolescent uproar and self-preoccupation end spontaneously when she reaches marriageable age and finds the right husband. This solution was not available to me. Medical school proved to be a valid *deus ex machina*. My self-image in relation to the world came into clearer focus.

I soon changed my mind and decided to be a psychiatrist, but this did not allow me to waive any part of the required curriculum. During my first two years I had to take courses in chemistry, physics, anatomy, and physiology. After the first two years we had to take examinations in the aforementioned preclinical subjects, as well as in histology and legal medicine. Only after passing these courses could a student go on to clinical studies.

Although I was not a devoted student, I got excellent marks on most of the exams. This was not always easy. For instance, my examiner in internal medicine was (at my own request) Professor Chwostek, who as a rule excluded all women students from his lectures and from his ward in the hospital. (Only seven women entered the School of Medicine when I did; only three of us finished.) Since Professor Chwostek's ban was technically illegal, he

1. Now, of course, known chiefly as an artist.

Wilhelm Rosenbach

Regina Fass Rosenbach

Hala at age 5

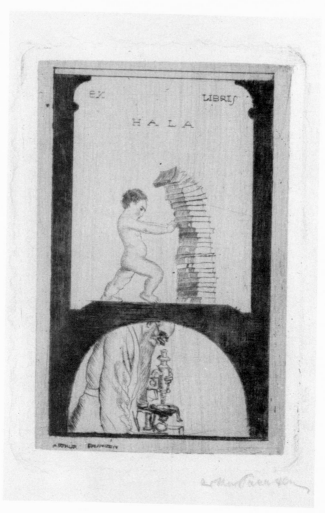

Bookplate designed for Helene Deutsch by her husband
(see page 122)

Gisela and her children: Irena, Arthur, and Leonard

Felix and Helene Deutsch at the time of their marriage in 1912

Freud in his study in Vienna with his dog Lün

Helene Deutsch in 1936 (*Egone Photo, Boston*)

On the farm at Babayaga

could not refuse to test a woman student if all the formalities were in order. Out of spite I made an excellent showing on the exam. He spat out the questions without looking at me, and addressed me as "Mr. Rosenbach." After it was over, he asked me in astonishment how I could have been so well-prepared. This still amuses me whenever I think of it.

One of my weak subects was histology. All of the students had discovered a way of making the examinations in this field easy: the janitor in the laboratory of the Histological Institute, for an appropriate tip, would tell us from which drawer the professor would take the specimens for the exam. His good offices were invaluable to several generations of medical students.

Vienna's medical school had a worldwide reputation and attracted many scholars and students from other countries, including America. I will mention only two of the professors who inspired my enthusiasm. One was Professor Meyer, who was able to make the usually boring subject of pharmacology fascinating. Another was the famous and brilliant Professor Tandler, whose extensive knowledge of sculpture, especially that of classical Greece, made his lectures on anatomy a pleasure to hear. He had the reputation of being more interested in his good-looking women students than his position as a teacher required. Some kind of sharp confrontation between us became inevitable.

I would sometimes arrive late at his lectures, which all students were required to attend. When I entered the lecture hall all heads would turn in my direction, neglecting the speaker. On one of these occasions, Tandler, visibly irritated, interrupted his lecture and said sardonically, "I'm waiting till the hearts of the students have calmed down."

Another time the two of us had a small *rencontre*. For our work in practical anatomy, we had cadavers assigned to us, four students per cadaver, two if it was a child's. When I received one of the small cadavers along with another student, Tandler asked the latter, in a voice loud enough for the whole class to hear, "Mr. X., would you like to have a child with Miss Rosenbach?"

He got what he wanted—gales of laughter—but I went to his office after class and declared to him in a solemn voice, "If anything like this ever happens again, I'll find ways. . . ."

But aside from these incidents and the examination with Professor Chwostek, I was taken seriously by everyone as a good student.

I was a wretched surgeon, however, and had to learn the obligatory material as best I could from my work on the cadaver. The famous Viennese surgeon Professor Eiselsberg noticed my lack of skill immediately. But when he saw my excellent record, he said to me, "I can pass you only on one condition: that you solemnly promise never to lift your knife against a human being."

The fragmentary and anecdotal character of these memories indicates how little meaning my medical studies had for me per se. I needed my status as a medical student primarily as something that could lend me an identity in this otherwise insecure period of my life. And I needed it for my father's sake, to give him the reassurance that I would soon be entering a respectable profession.

L.'s connection with the Socialist Party required him to take part in its international meetings. In 1910, during my summer vacation, the two of us attended the International Socialist Congress in Stockholm. This trip, which included a leisurely journey toward Sweden, was a turning point in my youth. What began as a pleasure jaunt ended in major emotional reorientation. For me the essence of the experience was being together with L. Although the certainty that we would soon separate weighed heavily on me, the journey to the Congress is one of the loveliest memories of my life.

We avoided the well-worn tourist routes and instead crossed from Germany into Sweden via the Gotha Canal, known to many from the romantic settings in Selma Lagerlöf novels. The mail ship on which we traveled down the canal would stop at the wonderfully clean and peaceful little towns, leaving bundles of packages and letters unguarded on the bank of the canal. We were told that it was unheard of for anyone to walk off with mail not addressed to him. It pleased me to hear this; my own poor fatherland was full of thieves, because of its poverty, and in Vienna one always locked even one's desk drawers.

In Norway I was intrigued by the reserved, even secretive character of the people. I understood it better when I saw the vast distances between settlements and also between individual isolated farms. Even a brief tourist's glance at this landscape makes Norwegian literature much more comprehensible.

After our canal trip our ship eventually dropped anchor in the country's northernmost town, Narvik. L. felt the landscape was depressing me, but that was not true. It was the town's similarity to Przemyśl. It was a Sunday, a band was playing on the *Ringplatz* and *"in dem kleinem Städtchen gingen auf und ab die Mädchen"* ("in the little town the girls stroll up and down"). In Narvik the small-town gallants stood leaning against the houses and watching the girls. In Przemyśl it was the officers, and we would put on our prettiest dresses and promenade. . . .

From Narvik we went by ship to the North Cape; I didn't go up the hill with the others to see the view of the Cape because someone had told me that at the top there was a refreshment stand! It was during this part of the journey that the ship was trapped for two or three days by icebergs. It was always daytime and the famous midnight sun was disturbing, though not nearly as glowing red as in the travel book pictures.

Wonderful as our voyage was, and rich with impressions, it also had its depressing elements. In some elegant hotel one evening (was it in Balholm?) young people were dancing and playing naïve outdoor games. I was not among them, of course, but I was their age and suddenly had the feeling that life had cheated me. I had never participated in such games at all, for at that early age I felt surrounded by the tragedy of my love. Here again both L. and I sensed the coming mood of parting.

The Congress itself was my first encounter with the larger world of socialism. I met most of the big names of the scientific-theoretical segment of the movement as well as those involved in practical and direct organization: Jaurès, Bebel, Kautsky, etc. These powers of the Party were true men! It was like a dream actually to see them and listen to their speeches. However, I learned soon enough that the world of socialism I had so idealized was torn by internal feuds, intrigues, splinterings. I wasn't well-versed enough in theory to comprehend the factional disputes; they aroused in me a sense of inferiority, and I humbly deferred to the arguments of those great men that I believed in. I recall that the Polish party, whose ideology I shared, was divided into a right and a left, and I felt a natural affinity for the left.

Meanwhile I was seeking models with whom I could identify; these could only be found among the feminine leaders. In all the crowd of women representing their different groups at the Congress, I found two who corresponded to the ego-ideal I needed. They were Rosa Luxemburg and Angelica Balabanoff. In this gathering that swarmed with famous men, both of these women were treated with significant respect, and their speeches had a strong, often decisive influence on the proceedings. I heard these speeches with awe.

I wanted to know more about these powerful women. I found out that Rosa Luxemburg was born into a Polish-Jewish bourgeois family, as I was, and that throughout her life she had maintained a close, typically Jewish attachment to her relatives. But when she was only fifteen, burning with indignation against the evils of society, she had joined the Socialist Party. It is interesting to note how she transferred her adolescent rebellion from her family to the whole of bourgeois society. Rosa Luxemburg might be considered a good subject for a psychoanalytical biography, but the scope of her activities and of her ideological battles and achievements would make it impossible to bring her under the microscope of psychoanalysis.

Young, inexperienced, but very talented, Rosa quickly developed all the qualities of a revolutionary. Her aggressive tendencies could be turned to constructive purposes in the service of her socialist aims. There was plenty of room for their release within the framework of the Party, to which she devoted her whole life. One continually heard rumors about her battles within the ranks—they could be personal as well as theoretical and from time to time brought about splits, easily traced to Rosa's intolerance. Her arguments often met opposition from the great theoreticians of the movement. Whether it was a matter of theory or strategy, Rosa usually won, because the power of her arguments and her unlimited devotion to the socialist cause were overwhelming. Also, her influence on the masses was immense. Her energies were not directed merely toward dissent and factionalism, but more toward welding together the various forces that were so apt to divide and weaken the Party. She worked hard for that stirring call: "Workers of the world, *unite!*"

She worked just as hard for women's political and economic equality and was a suffragette in the full, noble meaning of the word. During her whole life she remained unconditionally opposed to war, and her fanatical devotion to peace often brought her into conflict with powerful pro-war forces within the Party. But through her anti-war propaganda she was able to bring together divided groups of workers and liberals, even though her efforts to prevent World War I were in the end unsuccessful.

I met Rosa at the Congress. She took a sporadic interest in me because I was good-looking and obviously burning with adolescent devotion to the Party (which I believed would realize the ideals of the French Revolution not only for the workers but for the whole world). She regarded me as a naïve, enthusiastic child —indeed, in her attitude to me I felt something soft and perhaps motherly. This was not what I wanted. When we met, she always recognized me and asked questions about my work in the Party. My political allegiance was not to her faction, but we never spoke about it. I often wished to be like her, but I was realistic enough to know that this was impossible.

She was perhaps more intense in her emotions than the men,

and sometimes less controlled. But I noticed that during all the hostilities and quarrels her sex was never brought up as an argument against her. She was too great to be considered "only a woman," even by her enemies.

I would like to digress for a moment and compare Rosa to another woman who had a great influence on me in this period: Baroness Bertha von Suttner. This remarkable woman was a member of the Austrian aristocracy and among them she became a leader in the fight for peace. An outstanding propagandist, she had organized in Vienna and Berlin very active branches of the International Peace and Arbitration Association and written a best-selling anti-war novel, *Die Waffen Nieder (Lay Down Your Arms)*. By chance—she was answering a newspaper advertisement for a private secretary—she met Alfred Nobel, the inventor of dynamite, who was making a fortune manufacturing explosives for use in the Crimean War. Gradually she converted him to her pacifist views. It was largely because of her influence on Nobel that the Foundation, which he endowed in his will in 1895, included a prize for work on behalf of world peace. In 1905 Bertha herself became the first woman to receive this prize.

Restless, aggressive, ambitious, Bertha von Suttner did not resemble in the least one's image of the gentle, peace-loving woman —although psychoanalytic insight into her personality shows that her struggles for peace were a reaction-formation against her own aggressiveness. Despite their common aim, Bertha never acknowledged or respected the heroic struggles of the women working for world peace within the socialist movement. Preoccupied with her own ambitions, she ignored the existence of Rosa Luxemburg, although the two women were for a time both living in Vienna. This animosity was not surprising since Bertha's pacifism was based on a much less radical social philosophy than Rosa Luxemburg's. Indeed, Tolstoy once referred to *Lay Down Your Arms* as "the *Uncle Tom's Cabin* of the pacifist cause."

Angelica Balabanoff, whom I also met at the Congress, was almost a contemporary of Rosa Luxemburg. She had been working in a different way, in another part of the world and far from party strife, to help other human beings gain the rights they had been deprived of. She never attained Rosa's international popularity, and for a long time restricted her work to those who had never before been reached by socialist ideas—primarily the Italian railroad workers. Angelica left her wealthy aristocratic Russian family to take up the cause of the most neglected group of proletarians. While Rosa's rebellion was transferred outside the family circle, Angelica, like many adolescents of both sexes, began her rebellion inside the family. In her case it was a private revolution against her aristocratic mother, even though she owed to her mother the opportunity to develop her great linguistic talent. This hatred of her mother condemned her in her youth to a life of self-imposed poverty and suffering. She identified herself with the poor and the socially inferior as a reaction against her mother's upper-class intolerance and lack of humanity. She left home without any hesitation, and it appears that she never went back.

Though living in Russia at the time, she was not directly involved in the early stages of the Russian Revolution. It seems that during her juvenile rebellion she was more interested in the people's immediate suffering through exploitation than in making contact with other political revolutionaries. However, after the Revolution she became a secretary of the Communist International. Her later political career sounds like a fairy tale of ambitions fulfilled.

I met her again when she was the Soviet ambassador to Vienna —I didn't like her then. But at the beginning of her career she was inspiring. When she was ready to act, she did not look for a party to join but, on the contrary, for proletarians lacking the protection of an organization. These she found, especially among the railroad workers. She went to Italy, where her linguistic ability helped her immensely. Angelica also looked like an Italian working woman—a small dark-eyed brunette without the slightest resemblance to a Russian aristocrat.

Her power over the newly organized railroad workers was extraordinary. Here is a good example of their devotion to her. Once when Angelica was traveling to a peace meeting in Germany, she reached the local railroad station and found that there was only one train scheduled for Rome, where she had to change trains to get to Germany. A consultation with the railroad agent revealed that the Rome train would arrive too late for Angelica to make the necessary connection. Thereupon the devoted railroad worker re-routed the train in accordance with the needs of his beloved leader and Angelica arrived at the meeting in time.

Like Rosa Luxemburg, Angelica was constantly involved in the Party's inner conflicts, suffering more from these than from difficulties in the outside world. I think that all ideological movements fight on two fronts: there is the enemy outside and the enemy within.

Angelica's political life, like Rosa's, gave her the opportunity to channel her aggressions toward socially valuable goals. Her hostility, initially turned against her mother, later against opponents within the Party, was above all a weapon against the old social order. Both of these women are classic examples of the process of sublimation. Destructive impulses were harnessed to work for social justice and peace among nations.

By 1910 Angelica had become a very popular figure at all the international socialist conferences. Her linguistic genius made her sought-after as a simultaneous translator in three languages. The rhetorical style of her translations was often so brilliant that the audience was more impressed by the translator than by the original speaker, even if he was Jaurès, Van der Velde, or Kautsky.

Never had my inner frustration struck me as hard as it did at this Congress! I asked myself why I was not a leading woman like Rosa Luxemburg or Angelica Balabanoff. With my temperament, talent, and ambition, why hadn't I attained their status? I had had the opportunity; my connections with the Socialist Party had opened the way . . . but after setting out on it I had wandered off to the side.

This questioning was itself the first step toward the end of my relationship with L.; it took a year longer to complete the inevitable break. Once I had returned home from the Congress, I emerged from the intoxication of the experience into a mood of sober evaluation. I realized at last that my socialist zeal was fatally amalgamated with my love for the socialist leader. This realization cast a shadow on both my love and my social idealism. In my early adolescence I had longed for great experiences transcending the helpless dependence of love for *one* man. Meanwhile, as I ripened into womanhood, ideology and passionate love had become closely interwoven, with love dominating and swallowing up most of my creative endeavors. Thus, as I came to see after the 1910 Congress, my love was in conflict with my own ego-ideal, now re-stimulated and reinforced by meeting Rosa Luxemburg and Angelica Balabanoff.

The destructive force of my relationship with L. was invincible because the fantasy of self-sacrifice on behalf of society was simultaneously being played out in my erotic life. My suffering for and with L. had become the guiding element of my love. As I can see now, with the objectivity of an old person, the real expectations and demands of this relationship were transformed within my mind, as if by a kaleidoscope, into patterns of heroic resignation and sacrifice. It appears that in me the masochistic element was predominant, while for him it was the fantasy that had stayed with him since early youth of sacrificing himself as Christ did for the suffering of mankind. I could see this dream hidden beneath his sober and methodical political work in the service of his party. In me it had found more than a mere echo: my social idealism was a modus vivendi in my rebellion against the tyranny and reactionary attitudes of a mother whom I hated, just as his was initially rooted in hate for his capitalist father (I could see this even then). As I matured I gave up all active social rebellion—my love for L. outlasted it—but he remaind true to his political mission until the end of his life. In 1944 I read in the newspapers that he had died in London as Minister of Culture in the Polish government-in-exile.

The 1910 Stockholm Congress was the opening wedge, but it

was biology that finally resolved our impasse: I was ripe for motherhood, and the nature of our relationship made it out of the question. This realization pushed us toward a final parting. I turned all my energies back toward my medical work, which hopeless love, politics, and the constant emotional strain had caused me to neglect. And I satisfied some longings—which I had hidden even from my friend—for Vienna's music, theater, lovely books, and sometimes for pretty dresses. I escaped as often as I could to the *Burgtheater,* where the tradition of the great actor Kainz still lived on, and to the concert hall to hear the classical music that was one of Vienna's superb delights.

Yet I was aware that none of these things could make up for my emotional desolation, and felt that only a complete separation could help me recover from this painful relationship. I decided to use my privilege as a medical student to spend the last year of my studies at another university. I left Vienna for Munich, where I met Felix Deutsch.

VIII

Munich and the Wagner-Jauregg Clinic

EVEN BEFORE I met Felix Deutsch, I had a deep interest in human beings in general, their loves, hates, errors, and sufferings. I had been moved to seek an answer to their mystery in medicine. Actually it was in the study of psychiatry that I expected to find the answer, for I felt that only a thin partition separates the psychically normal from the diseased. My husband's work was to conform and strengthen this intuition.

What I learned from my own experience, however, was that the essential element in understanding another person is the ability, as Sartre said in *Les Mots,* to "walk the paths another has walked," in other words to identify oneself with that person. Only thus can insight be gained into another's soul. There is another truth that is grasped only through direct experience: people appear to be inscrutable because they wear various disguises that lead us astray. Even a person's behavior does not reveal the true man at all times.

An episode that took place many years ago taught me more than many a psychological paper. I was worried about the health of someone who was close to me. Restless and sleepless, I got up out of bed one night and set out for his house, stealing on foot down the poorly lighted streets. I knew I would have to pass a corner where there was a drugstore and that this corner was the regular hangout of an aggressive gang with a very bad reputation. We always avoided parking the car near there—this gang specialized in auto thefts. And sure enough, as I approached the spot, two fellows tougher-looking than the rest sprang out of the group and placed themselves on either side of me. One of them, with a menacing smile, mockingly offered me his arm. From sheer passive helplessness, since I was so preoccupied with my own troubles, I took his arm. And so we marched, three abreast, toward my destination. When I stopped in front of the house, they stayed by my side, and when I had finished my inspection—I only wanted to see whether a light was on in a certain room—and turned back toward home, the same young man again offered me his arm, this time with a certain air of gallantry. My escorts walked me all the way home. Before I went inside, they both said good night, and the first one added: "Lady, don't go out alone at night, it's dangerous." I saw then the kind person beneath the threatening exterior. I would have liked to find out more about him, but he gave me no opportunity. The path of empathetic identification was open only from my end. I'd been won over, but the two young men wanted to know nothing more about me, as though I had surprised them in some naughty deed!

The science of psychology had already beckoned to me during my first two years of medical school in Vienna, and I had devoted more time than the curriculum required to the study of psychiatry. (I must admit that my attraction to this field soon made me forget even my modest knowledge of medicine.) Now in Munich, in flight from my saddening break with L., I found myself at the University's medical school studying psychiatry under Professor Kräpelin.

I used that spring of 1911 to do research in the laboratory for experimental psychology. The theme of this research was "The

Role of the Emotions in Memories Recalled by Association."
This work was brought to a stage of only relative completion,
and I don't know what became of it later. But I am certain that
it was a harbinger of my turn toward psychoanalysis.

In Munich I met my future husband. I was sitting in the students' section, where I was known as "Rosenbachowska" (the
Polish version of my German name). He was sitting at the side of
the world-famous internist Professor Friedrich Müller, with whom
he was studying that year on a fellowship. It was a *coup de
foudre*. Felix succeeded in getting a mutual friend to introduce
us. This was the final and definitive end of my previous love
affair. I felt like a free soul for the first time in many years. I
remember that after our first hike together in the Bavarian
mountains Felix and I had to come home in a crowded train. I
had a grandiose feeling of liberation and I exclaimed, "The air is
clear!" He didn't understand me, for in fact the air was thick
with smoke and the smell of the tourists' sweat. This sense of
psychic "clear air" lasted during the whole fifty-two years of our
married life. Everyone who knew him had the same feeling about
him—that is, the good people! The others found him "naïve."

The year 1912 was both an emotional and a professional mile-
stone in my life. It was the year of our marriage and the year I
received my medical degree. This degree was the second step in
my social liberation, the first one being my *Abitur*. Even more
gratifying than the academic success was the fact that although
my father couldn't attend the commencement ceremony, L. was
in the audience that consisted mostly of parents of the graduates.
My father could not have found a better substitute.

In my profession I had at last reached the point where my
real interests had been leading. With my diploma in hand, the
way was clear. There was little attraction for me in medicine as
such, and I chose to devote the following years entirely to psychiatry. I had to give up the usual training program of prospective doctors, which would have been useful in orienting me in
various other fields but didn't really interest me very much. An

academic career was out of the question for women at this time.
(I no longer remember exactly when women won equal treatment in this regard at the University of Vienna.)

For six years, from 1912 to 1918, I worked as a full-time assistant at the Wagner-Jauregg psychiatric clinic in Vienna. Any
official, permanent appointment of a woman by the Austrian
government was then unheard of, though the head of the clinic
was actively on my side. These formalities remained fairly unimportant to me. Less trivial was the fact that the assistantship
at the clinic was an unpaid position, and thus a luxury a poor
doctor could ill afford. Two factors eased the situation somewhat: I had gone through periods of poverty before and going
hungry was nothing new; and during the war my appointment as
a military doctor meant better than average pay.

Going hungry during my student days in Vienna comes back
to me, I admit, with some nostalgia. I recall standing with other
starving fellow students in a long line in front of the Mensa
Academica of the University waiting for the opening of the doors,
tantalized by the wonderful smell of the hamburger with sauerkraut. By the end of the month it was mostly just sauerkraut, as
hamburger was a luxury. To be sure, such spells of hunger had
something theatrical about them (how I enjoyed the rôle of the
starving girl student) because, in the first place, I could have
written home to my parents for money any time I felt like it,
and in the second place, all kinds of interesting ways for me to
earn money had turned up. But during the war years hunger was
only too real. Everyone went hungry; the doctors had it slightly
better because the rations for hospital patients and personnel
were generally adequate. My husband would come home in the
evening carrying bags containing what was supposed to be his
portion but was enough to feed the two of us.

Our professional situations were very different. When we met,
Felix Deutsch was already a brilliant and outstanding physician,
while I was still only a student. By 1912 I had my diploma but
was still in the initial stages of my chosen career. To be sure I

was soon named a military doctor, but fundamentally the war years, thanks to my energy and desire for knowledge, were *learning* years, in the best sense of the word.

At the clinic, I found Dr. Wagner-Jauregg quite willing to set up an experimental laboratory. But meanwhile my own interest in experimentation had dwindled, and I wanted no more equipment than a stopwatch! Nevertheless my experiments were, if not revolutionary, quite interesting in a modest way. I can't remember now whether they were published. My strongest recollection is of a fascinating long-term observation of an otherwise normal woman patient who remained mute for months at a time. My guess was that she had something to conceal and I expected to bring her out of her stupor into life and consciousness. The outcome was that she became attached to me and regained her speech as a kind of gift to me. I didn't insist on knowing her secret, but the experience reinforced my belief in the healing forces of love. Today all this seems banal and prosaic, but at the time it was a discovery.

Since I thought that my future psychiatric work would be with children, I went to the famous pediatric clinic of Dr. Clemens Pirquet and joined the work of Dr. Lazar with mentally defective children. As yet little was known about the emotional disturbances of children, and most of the cases seemed to be intellectual deficiencies: idiocy, mongolism, etc. After half a year of not very productive work, I returned to the Wagner-Jauregg Clinic.

At this time a "sensational discovery" of Abderhalden was very much in vogue. His thesis was that certain diagnoses could be made by comparing the colors of the liquid in two test tubes, to one of which the serum of the patient had been added. The color would be pink or bluish-purple according to whether the patient was sick or well.[1] But the colors were often so pale that I myself couldn't tell for sure what they were. So I had to wander

1. The chemical process in this procedure was complicated even for the clinical observer.

through the clinic with my test tubes, asking everyone I ran into —doctors, cleaning women, even patients: "Is this pink or blue?" only to decide eventually that the correct answer was my own original guess. This research method did not prove very valuable, and was definitely a waste of my time.

I have the impression that with time Dr. Wagner-Jauregg came to value my work highly. In his work with patients suffering from progressive paralysis due to syphilis he found that infection with malaria was an effective treatment. This discovery attracted great attention at the time and brought Wagner-Jauregg the Nobel Prize. He entrusted to me the important task of transferring the malaria serum and observing the subsequent behavior of several patients. I remember one of the first cases: a poor cleaning woman who continued to show her symptoms of paralysis even after the treatment. All the other doctors were enthusiastic about this so-called success. I alone remained silent, for I could see no truly significant change in her condition. I believe that Wagner-Jauregg respected the honesty of my work with these patients, for of his own accord he promised me an appointment as an assistant in the clinic, and he carried out this promise as far as he could. As I have mentioned, my sex precluded an official appointment. When Dr. Paul Schilder came back from the front —he was a likely male candidate for the position of assistant— Wagner-Jauregg found himself in an embarrassing position. He soon recognized in Schilder a very original and productive spirit, but he was aware of his promise to me and hesitated to displace me in his favor. I understood the situation and kept my own counsel. I was content to stay on at the clinic even without an official title, for it always had extraordinarily instructive patients whom I was free to observe and to treat, whatever my position was.

Wagner-Jauregg rejected psychoanalysis completely. His whole personality was too deeply committed to the rational, conscious aspects of life. Actually he never discussed psychoanalysis, at least in the presence of his staff, and limited his criticism to mocking asides. He knew that I was interested in it and had read all of Freud's writings that had come out so far. While making his rounds at the clinic, he often made sarcastic comments when he noticed that I had spent a longer time than usual with a patient. He could even go so far as to ask that patient, "Well, did Dr. Deutsch manage to convince you that you want to have a child by your father?" Yet, beneath all his opposition, one could see that he felt a fundamental respect for Freud. Naturally the ambitious professors around Wagner-Jauregg took pains to disparage Freud. But he usually disappointed them by ignoring their remarks.

For the duration of the war, most of the male doctors were drafted to do their military duty with the reserves, and many were sent to the front. This left Professor O. Pötzl and me to share between us the heavy workload of the clinic. We had some doctors assigned to us, but they were aged general practitioners with very little knowledge of psychiatry. Pötzl himself was not too easy to deal with—he was short-tempered and impatient—but on the other hand extremely gifted and erudite. I learned a great deal from him. Intellectually he had an affinity for psychoanalysis. He was too intelligent to accept the scornful attitude of the official psychiatric establishment.[1]

The self-reliance demanded of me in this emergency situation formed an important part of my education. We were working round-the-clock shifts during this time; I was required to make quick and accurate diagnoses, and thus virtually to determine the fate of the female patients. I also had the opportunity, in the beginning at least, to work with the most hopeless patients, the ones who had locked up their entire emotional lives deep within them, unable either to give love or to accept it. They would lie there in their beds, motionless and mute, as if dead, until after a period of "observation" they were judged unpromising for fur-

1. Pötzl's intolerant attitude toward the soldiers sent from the front for psychiatric observation on the suspicion of malingering is a dark chapter in the history of psychiatry in Vienna.

ther research, given the ominous diagnosis "stupor," and sent on to an institution for incurables.

Disregarding the opinion of the other doctors and staff that I was crazy, I often refused for a long time to give up on patients suffering from stupor. What I accomplished by my efforts did not fall short of my expectations. One example stays in my memory: after I had spent many days at the bedside of an "incurable" stupor victim, frequently whispering "I love you" into her ear, one day she suddenly seized my hand, pressed it to her heart, and smiled at me. This was a huge victory! I am sorry to say that soon after that she had to give up her bed to some more hopeful case and be transferred to an institution for incurables. My colleagues were sure that I had wasted my time, but I knew I had not. I had learned that one can penetrate the thickest wall of morbid narcissism if one is armed with a strong desire to help and a corresponding warmth.

Still, doubts were of course inevitable. Was it worthwhile to give so much of my limited time to one single person, or to lavish so much interest and warmth on a patient doomed to chronic insanity? And in the end, what did I know about her? Perhaps she was happier in her unexpressed, silent madness than the patient occupying the next bed over, suffering from depression and complaining loudly. Despite my occasional successes, I strongly sensed my own inadequacy and began to direct my attention more toward the organizational aspects of the work at the clinic. This was especially appreciated by the staff of nurses, sensitive beings who were conscious that the psychiatric treatment of the patients themselves was often rather hampered by the presence of so many research-minded, ambitious lecturers and professors. I myself had to complain about the lack of guidance from the more experienced doctors. But gradually I discovered that my very isolation and the necessity to take responsibility for my actions fostered my professional growth enormously. And as for practical experience, I gained it rapidly through the help of the wise old head nurse, Mrs. M., who had more to teach me about the mentally ill than the professors with their Latin diagnoses.

It was said that during the period when I was helping with administrative matters, the patients were better cared for and cleaner than ever before. I was the only one who felt dissatisfied. I was unhappy that I could help patients so very little. But at least I wrote good case histories. Long afterward, doctors from younger generations would say to me: "We learned much more from your case histories than we could have learned from other methods of teaching, about those patients who were repeatedly committed to the clinic."

As the war went on, further work with individual "hopeless" cases became impossible. We received hundreds of new patients from the overflowing military hospitals, and beds were sorely needed for the latest victims of the war-beast. War is war, but despite many points of similarity between warfare then and now, there are also crucial differences. Our weapons have grown "more reliable" and if our young fighters of today do not understand the *why* of a certain war, they can protest and demonstrate against it. The war victims who came into our clinic—naïve young peasants from the Slavic provinces (Serbia, the Ukraine, and Poland)—couldn't even read the falsified reports that came in from the front and hadn't, moreover, the least idea of what they were fighting for.

I was most upset by the victims of the cholera epidemic that decimated our forces at the front. They occupied hastily prepared rooms in the old mental hospital and died in great droves, in the face of the doctors' desperate efforts to save them with massive transfusions. They lay beyond my medical specialty, and they do not belong in my personal story, yet I can never forget them. Remembering them still arouses my anger at the exploitation of human lives by our society in past years and in the present. Indirectly, they added a great deal to my personal wisdom, for I am a woman and identification with others is characteristic of my sex. Through this painful empathy I learned that there is no greater human suffering to undergo than the degradation of one's personal dignity. Lying on their hard military pallets, reminded by their surroundings that they were expected to die a hero's death in battle for the fatherland instead of having to wallow in their own stinking excrement, these dying soldiers were beyond my help and indeed beyond what I could bear. They are deeply fixed in my memory as representing the terrible suffering of mankind.

IX

Marriage and Motherhood

AFTER AN INFORMAL engagement lasting about a year, Felix and I decided to get married. The conventions of our social and professional milieu as well as practical considerations all pointed in this direction. Although I had liberal social principles, I was no fanatic believer in free love, and besides, after so many years of reckless disregard of my parents' feelings, I genuinely wanted to set their minds at rest about me. We limited our wedding to a civil ceremony with two witnesses who at our request sent a confirming telegram to my parents. I had satisfied my conscience, but it also gave me deep pleasure to know that they could now be reassured that I had reached a peaceful harbor on my life's journey.

We spent the next few years occupied with our respective professional interests, I at the Wagner-Jauregg Clinic, my husband engrossed in his hospital work and scientific research. (There is no branch of internal medicine to which he has not made some contribution.) These years were not free from conflicts, which sometimes even threatened the harmony of our marriage. I infected my husband with my own psychic problems and often caused him mental unrest which, fortunately, he could keep from interfering with his work. Professional satisfactions compensated for the discords that could not be directly resolved. And we stayed together and did not waver in our love and solidarity.

The richness of Felix's personality could sometimes be an enigma to others. To me it never was, since to me he was, simply, Felix, and I regarded the abundance of his talents as a natural gift of God. I am happy that our son and grandsons seem to have inherited some of his qualities.

Felix never lost the "naïveté" I spoke of earlier. It was miraculous how well he combined the detachment of the scientist with a warm interest in his patients as people and an intense preoccupation with their emotional problems. Though immersed in numerous scientific researches as well as in his artistic pursuits, he was no stranger to the everyday world. Ordinary human beings were close to him, especially those who were suffering. He was for many the "born doctor."

He was one of the first men in medical science to abandon the psychic-physical duality; he sought for both elements in every manifestation of illness. His work in psychosomatic medicine demonstrated how psychic processes are mobilized under the influence of somatic pressure, and, vice versa, what power emotions can have over organic disease. His thorough knowledge of physiology and medicine did not prevent him from recognizing the powerful role of anxiety in the formation of bodily symptoms—anxiety which is diagnosed and conquered not by laboratory tests but by psychological intuition and knowledge of human beings.

The genesis of Felix's interest in psychosomatic ailments was so very typical of him! Though a research scientist and a scholar, he was apt to find his inspiration in simple human experiences. There were several incidents that spurred his interest in the influence of the psyche on bodily functions, but I remember especially the woman patient of his who had come to him with the symptoms of a serious heart condition. He treated her for her symptoms with the means he had at his disposal as an internist, but he was quite sure that this woman would not begin to react positively to the treatment until her only son came back from the front. It was clear that the woman's anxiety would counteract the good effects of any medical treatment.

The nature of his research of course soon directed his interest toward psychoanalysis. He had known Freud and begun reading his publications even before I did, but his definitive connection with the discipline came later, after I had already established my identity as a psychoanalyst. From that time on, he too lived in the atmosphere of the great revolution created by Freud, and took an active part in it. By then he had already broken through the dividing line between the somatic and the psychic and had become, as Freud said, the "liaison officer" between medicine and psychoanalysis.

Our disagreements were often in the professional field, and usually he was right. I was convinced, for example, that one could be a good analyst without having had any medical training. He believed that therapeutic work with neurotic patients required a thorough acquaintance with somatic as well as psychic disorders. To Felix, analysis was the most exact of sciences; for me it represented an ongoing process of revolution. And yet we were united in our understanding of Freud and of the world-shaking implications of psychoanalysis.

Felix continued to publish numerous books and articles on internal medicine, which were highly regarded in the medical community. He lived in the ecstasy of the discoverer: he learned the language of the body and spoke of each organ as part of a unity. He was an analytic scientist possessed of the all-important ability to synthesize. In fact, in his research he used a method that was a special, abbreviated application of the psychoanalytic method of free association. He called it "associative anamnesis." [1]

1. See Felix Deutsch and William Murphy, *The Clinical Interview* (New York: International Universities Press, 1955).

The criticism directed at him by some of his colleagues in internal medicine had a certain amount of negative influence on his practice, but generally the enormous public confidence he enjoyed remained constant. To be sure, there was a period when psychiatrists claimed he had little understanding of psychiatry because he was not one of them, while at the same time his colleagues questioned how such an outstanding internist could be anything besides an internist. One of them once asked him why he had given up medicine, and he exclaimed in surprise, "But I've never given it up!"

The announcement that he would read a paper to the Society of Internal Medicine on the influence of psychic symptoms on organic processes was received with tolerant curiosity. The audience in the elegant lecture hall of the medical faculty of the University of Vienna included most of the leading internists of the day. During the lecture a noticeably cool atmosphere set in, and I believe there was no discussion, or a very perfunctory one, afterwards. The hostile silence persisted even on the grandiose staircase as I left the hall, without Felix, and mingled with the audience on the way out. No one knew who I was. In the subdued atmosphere I heard someone comment to his neighbor apropos of this precedent-breaking lecture: *"Cherchez la femme!"* I never mentioned it to Felix, for it would have wounded him more than anything else. He wanted to be independent of me in his professional sphere. And he was.[1]

The reader is quite likely asking a logical question at this point: Weren't there problems involving the division of sex roles in such a marriage of two professional people? Yes, there were, but they were always solved before they were allowed to exert any real influence on our relationship or on our individual goals. In general, as I can see quite clearly from my own experience and from others, such problems are not at all difficult to

1. I will not enter more fully into a discussion of my husband's professional work because an extensive biography of him which emphasizes this aspect of his life has been written by his most outstanding collaborator, Sanford Gifford.

solve; they don't even exist as long as the more complicated human relationship is not confused with a sociological one. When one speaks of the difficulties and conflicts of modern married life, household problems as such play only a secondary role, in my opinion. The crucial factor is emotional energies and drives, aroused by social progress, which have to be incorporated into a new way of life.

For example, Felix had learned dietetic cooking for the sake of his patients, but he refused completely to become a domestic helper. I saw in that an expression of "masculine protest" and in retaliation, I guess, I tried to involve him in discussions of household affairs. He sympathized with my worries, and I even remember him walking around our apartment with a tube of household cement, trying to smooth out the cracks in the walls, but he never let himself become really involved.

We had a good mutual understanding—no, he understood me better than I understood him. His tenderness for me was never reduced by the press of his work or lack of time. I might be able to give many, many examples of it, if an almost unconquerable inhibition were not holding me back. He never felt that exotic flowers were too lavish a present, or that traveling in a certain style was too extravagant for me. Even after the storms of erotic love were behind us, our deep love never diminished. He liked women and had many good friends among them, but this never made me jealous.

Felix never resented the fact that I sometimes interrupted his work. Yet in spite of this tolerance, I was astonished again and again by the huge amount of work he accomplished. And furthermore, though preoccupied with intense professional and scientific activity, he had ample time left over to cultivate his artistic talents. He played the piano, composed, painted, and wrote poems for children to express his love for them.

He was a real musician. Before entering college he had been forced to make a choice between his two chief interests: whether to study medicine or music. He told me that this choice had been determined by necessity. Ever since his father's death when he was about eight years old, his family (mother, older brother, and a younger sister) had been in a rather precarious financial position. He wanted to have the means to support his mother as soon as possible. Thus it was bound to happen that medicine became the reality and music the dream, but a dream he never gave up.

Sometimes he didn't play for weeks. The piano became a taboo object, to be avoided like a danger. Then some afternoon, with the passion of a man giving up a long abstinence, he would come upstairs from his office earlier than usual and spend hours improvising music that was *Felix*. When he got up from the piano to answer my call to supper, his shirt would be wringing wet, his eyes glowing. He would apologize like a young boy that he'd be a little late, since he had to change clothes, ". . . it's the music."

In his musical taste he remained true to the great masters Mozart and Beethoven; Mahler was also high on his list. It may be that his preferences had been influenced by personal experiences. In the case of Mozart there were our strolls in the Vienna woods, which took us to places that the composer had often visited as a little boy with his father. I think of the warm summer nights when we rambled over those hills and then, below, often got a little tipsy at the *Heuriger,* a romantic little open-air coffeehouse; and of the ride home on the overcrowded streetcar, often *die letzte Blaue,* singing German songs with the other passengers. I wasn't pure Viennese as Felix was, but I loved to dance to the Strauss waltzes. The *Heuriger* was always associated in our minds with well-loved guests from abroad whom we took there to enjoy its characteristic Viennese atmosphere.

We were happy—but my old friend and enemy, the restless desire for excitement and, above all, for learning and achievement, did not let me fully enjoy what we possessed. "The air was clear," but somehow I longed for storms. This longing was not silent and from time to time forced me to get away. It was my own inner battle for liberation, no longer raging, but now and then making ghostlike noises. I always wanted to learn something that could only be learned somewhere else—I wanted to repeat my adolescent flight from home. Or to say it even more simply, I longed for new longings. And I used the same rationalization as before: I wanted to learn. I had my freedom, and yet I missed my old battles for it! However, when I was away I would wait impatiently for letters from Felix.

My recollections of those years do not flow freely, and I have to rely on reconstructions. I know that I went away to Munich, where Felix and I first met, to spend a few months. I enjoyed the refreshing clarity of Kräpelin's lectures and the work in the well-organized laboratory for experimental psychology. I came back in the spring, when Vienna is at its best. At that time we had been married for four years. Our feeling of unity crystallized into a definite wish to have a child.

Even before I conceived, I had the fear that I would never have a child, and this fear did not subside during my pregnancy. I could not believe that my quite normal pregnancy would really result in a child. These anxieties were not unique. "Each woman brings into her pregnancy certain emotional factors and conflicts which come into relation with her condition."[1] I did have joy and happy expectations, but these were mixed with panic, as if long-buried forces could still have their old destructive power.

These difficulties were alleviated by the grace of destiny. A dear friend of mine, whom I called the "goddess of serenity," had become pregnant a month before me, and through identification with her my motherhood changed its character. Through a psychological impact on biological forces, my desire for a child was fulfilled: my friend gave birth to her son one month later than she had expected—just when my pregnancy reached its term. My son was born six hours after hers. My happiness was without bounds. But it was not until I heard him crying and took him in my arms that I really believed in his existence.

Felix had to postpone his desire for a daughter until the next

1. Helene Deutsch, *The Psychology of Women,* vol. 2 (New York: Grune & Stratton, 1944) p. 127.

generation, but that generation played a trick on him. Instead of a granddaughter he was given two grandsons to love. And he did love them very deeply. I of course remembered the saying of the Talmud: "A woman becomes a woman only when she has given birth to a boy." I also thought of Freud's remark that there is only one relationship than can be free of ambivalence, the one between mother and son. I would emphasize the *can be,* because, if taken as a rule, this pronouncement has many exceptions. A son's Oedipal love, reinforced in adolescence, often makes him a fugitive; sometimes he flees and does not return. Also the strongly narcissistic element in mother love (*"my* son") makes the mother prone to reactions of disappointment and the son to resentful hostility.

The presence of a child of either sex always complicates the home situation, especially on the emotional level. The mother-child relationship weighs heavily on the emotional structure of the family. And it goes without saying that it often changes a woman's attitudes toward her chosen profession. It was seldom the household that threatened to come between me and my career. It was my motherhood, not in the actual time it required, but in its libidinous demands. I have always tried to deny this fact, but my husband expressed it without words in an *Ex Libris* he ordered for me, which is reproduced in the illustration section. My situation was eased by his willingness to give up much of his "man's role" in order to provide me with some leisure and time for my professional work. To him it was merely a way of helping, and he did these tasks with untiring patience.

Felix had not been called to the front, but assigned to provide for the medical needs of *eight* private hospitals in addition to his regular duties as head of the department of internal medicine at the Wiedener Hospital. (These newly created hospitals for war victims were supported by the female relatives of the Kaiser. In the spirit of the Austrian monarchy, these royal women did not remain idle in the crisis: they worked as nurses in their own hospitals and carried out their tasks with thoroughness and devotion.) Felix was therefore more and more overwhelmed by work, and so was I. The problem of taking care of an infant became ever more difficult. While trying to cope with the heavy professional workload caused by the war, I always had the painful suspicion that I was depriving both my son Martin and myself of a rich source of happiness, the mother-child closeness that is most significant to a baby during the first two years. I loved my child deeply, but the two of us could only occasionally experience the blessing of the mother-child bond with all its tenderness and care. My motherly feelings, moreover, were disturbed by anxieties of a deeply neurotic character concerning my little son. It became clear that they were rooted in the infantile neurosis that had made me wait up at night for my father's return, convinced that something horrible had happened to him.

Meanwhile, in spite of all complications, I was functioning better than ever in my work. This was also true later on; a list of my publications during the years of Martin's childhood shows that my scientific work was not suffering. As I look back, I can see that whenever the door to *sublimation* was open to me, I was much happier as a wife and mother. And vice versa: when something in my personal life interfered with my scientific productivity, I was less happy and more aggressive in my whole attitude toward my environment.

Professional responsibilities gave me—or so I thought—the right to engage a nurse. Old Paula was dependability itself and seemed to be a perfect mother substitute. My thinking on this was not rational. Motherhood is a full-time occupation, today as it was then, especially during the first two years of a child's life, if not in a literal sense, at least in terms of the psychic energy we call mother love. I expressed this viewpoint many years ago in *The Psychology of Women* (1944). Even then many of my female contemporaries called me reactionary.

I myself did not follow my own good judgment. Paula practically insisted on taking upon herself the responsibilities of a good, experienced mother during the two years she was with us. Her

chief stipulation was that I abdicate a great part of my motherhood and become a sort of mirage. I was to appear and disappear
like an affectionate visitor. Of course I insisted on nursing the
child myself. Milk was hard to come by in Vienna then, and even
a not too productive nurse like me was acceptable. I spent a large
part of the day in the excruciating business of providing the
amount of mother's milk needed. The baby thrived on it; I,
however, was becoming physically and psychically drained. My
kind and concerned husband found a solution: in the midst of
the war shortages he managed to acquire two goats from a farmer
in a rural area near Vienna. He traded a piano for them (he had
two) and personally brought them into Vienna from the country,
going part of the way on foot. The goats grazed and fought in
the courtyard of the Wagner-Jauregg Clinic during the day. The
clinic gave me an extra room next to my office where I installed
my son and his nurse; and Martin's two new substitute nurses,
the goats, met with his complete satisfaction.

When it comes to a discussion of the conflict between a
woman's professional work and her motherhood, I can say, grown
wiser through my own experience, that in the period of my
son's childhood, this conflict could be worked out only on an
individual basis, and with many compromises. Since then social
progress, while not eliminating all difficulties connected with
motherhood, has increased women's opportunities as active members of society outside the home. A large measure of freedom and
equality has been achieved; more is coming. I welcome all progress in the direction of women's liberation with pleasure, but
also with a silent, sad realization: though woman is different now,
she is forever the same, a servant of her biological fate, to which
she has to adjust her other pursuits.

In any case, war, the horrible despot that ignores all biological,
social, and psychological problems in pursuit of its own deadly
aims, automatically solved for me the problem of women's proper
place in society. I was a doctor and doctors were needed; I had
no choice. I don't mean to say that there was an enforced demand

for women workers, only that I felt a definite obligation connected with my profession. Financial considerations also came into play; war service was very well paid.

On the other hand, in spite of my sense of professional obligation, my work as a war doctor evoked deep guilt feelings: I was part of the war although my ideology was strongly anti-war. Sometimes I felt like a war criminal basking in the sun of my own importance as a woman doctor. I was even a war profiteer, better paid than regular physicians! Even now I experience a trace of guilt and have to remind myself of my individual helplessness and other alleviating factors. For instance, my position as a woman doctor had great positive value as a step toward the social equality of women, in spite of the suffering it caused my parents, the deprivation of important years of motherhood, and the fact that my work kept me apart from my husband for so much of the time.

By the time I had finished my year of obligatory service in neurology, the war was over. My husband and I felt its after-effects like everyone else. Although doctors in the hospitals were somewhat better provided for than the general public, hunger was widespread. Together with the deceptive slogan "Never again war!" a passive mood of "What now?" set in. Felix and I shared it with many others.

Often during Martin's childhood and youth, I thought to myself, "How glad I am that you're *his* son!" For Felix was a miraculous father. Martin from the first had an exceptionally strong love for him. Even in situations in which a child usually calls for his mother, he turned more often to Felix than to me. At night he used to call "Uhu!" and this became a name for Felix in our family circle and among our friends. I always found it touching that our grandsons gave this name their sanction by calling Felix "Gruhu" (Grand-Uhu).

I've never seen another man who could so readily identify himself with children and join in their interests as Felix. I called him the Pied Piper; whenever he visited anywhere the children would talk about him for a long time afterwards and ask, "Where's Flix?" He always had some candy in his pocket for the children in our neighborhood. Once when I suggested to him that the mothers might not like to see their children taking candy from a stranger, he answered in surprise, "But *I'm* not a stranger!" To me these words say so much! No, he was not a stranger, to children or to those that he could help.

He was the most mature man I have ever known, and one of the few who could have claimed the superiority of the wise man. Yet he could himself be little more than a child when he played with children. This strong man often awakened the most motherly feelings in me. After Martin I had no other children, but he and his father filled my emotional life to the brim.

Martin was a sensitive and highly gifted child, but despite his precocious development he remained psychologically normal. He talked and walked very early, and his speech was almost from the beginning that of a much older child. He was a rapid and eager reader, and began at an early age to show an interest in the exact sciences. It soon became obvious that his future lay there. At first it was mostly chemistry; then, from age ten on, it was physics. On his own initiative and without our knowledge, he made frequent visits to a physics laboratory, where he was taken seriously in spite of his youth.

Once when he was about ten years old, he wanted to see a certain scientific demonstration at a lecture hall that was not open to anyone under the age of fifteen. My husband managed to get him in by promising to hold him in his lap during the presentation. In the discussion that followed, someone asked a question nobody could answer—it had something to do with the formation of rain. At this point, up sprang Martin from his father's lap, and provided the right answer. I could tell many such stories, but shall try not to be a typical mother basking in the achievements of her children and grandchildren.

Martin enjoyed being alone, but he was in no way an isolated child. He always had friends and from adolescence on was a leader in his circle—a circle that was definitely coeducational. He was a good student and in high school was well above the level of his class, a fact that sometimes brought him into difficulties with those teachers who had rather limited intellectual capacities.

But, much as I would enjoy it, I am not writing a biography of my son; he would not approve. Suffice it to say that the intense and positive relationship between Felix and Martin continued through the years. It found its expression more through science than music; in later times, a great part of our family Sunday dinners was taken up by scientific discussions between these two men, to the great disappointment of the grandchildren, waiting to play with "Gruhu."

Felix's love of music later became an important element in his relationship with his grandsons. It was in the period of their childhood, I think, that he most actively exercised his artistic talents. During the last years of his life, his taste in music changed and his interest in painting grew stronger; he began to cultivate atonal music as well as modern art. He was especially drawn to Arnold Schönberg's compositions, Rodin's sculpture, and the painting of Kandinsky.

It becomes increasingly painful for me to write about the person whom I cannot and probably never will cease to mourn. Let me, then, pass to the more objective story of my work with Freud and the founding of the psychoanalytic movement in Vienna.

X

Freud[1]

MY FIRST confrontation with Freud was in 1907, when I became acquainted with his analysis of dreams by reading Wilhelm Jensen's novel *Gradiva* (1905) and Freud's interpretation of it (1907).[2] Even then, my mind was more attuned to the beauties of literature than to the arcana of scientific problems. When some years later my dear and learned friend Josef Reinhold[3] (a student and assistant of the philosopher Friedrich Jodl) sent me *The Interpretation of Dreams* (published in 1900) and

1. I would like to thank Anna Freud for her help in correcting mistakes of my memory in this chapter.
2. "Delusions and Dreams in Jensen's *Gradiva*", in *The Complete Works of Sigmund Freud*, transl. J. Strachey, Hogarth Press, 1959, vol. 9 pp. 7–93, with Freud's postscript to the 2nd edition pp. 94–5; originally published as "Die Wahn und die Träume in W. Jensens *Gradiva*", *Gesammelte Werke*, 1907.
3. I was separated from this lifelong friend when I left Vienna for America in 1934, but he was among those loved ones whom I tried to bring over to the United States. I secured for him a non-quota visa and a professorship of medicine at one of the smaller universities, but I was unable to persuade him to abandon his research at the well-known Gräfenberg sanitarium in Czechoslovakia, and his connection as physician and personal friend of Jan Masaryk. With the visa in his pocket he was killed by the Nazis.

Psychopathology of Everyday Life (published in 1904), I was already prepared to accept Freud's new theories. Apparently my many years of conventional work at the clinic had not entirely atrophied my judgment: I knew at once what significance these books had for science. I was very excited; I read all day and all night.

Freud's study of the effects of cocaine and his collaboration in the researches of the highly respected Professor Josef Breuer were anticipations of his later discoveries, which soon made him an object of dislike for many, and of guarded fascination for others. Freud himself sensed his great mission. Behind the modest satisfaction of "I have a therapy" lay the inner realization that he was about to "knock the world out of its old rut." When he was only seventeen years old, Freud had confided half-jokingly in a letter to his friend Emil Fluss that he had the fantasy of being a genius. Many adolescents have such a fantasy, but in Freud's case it was a prediction of truth.

What came to be known as the psychoanalytic movement originated under the leadership of Freud himself. For me, the analytic world consisted at first of Freud and myself; then of Freud and the Vienna Psycho-Analytic Society; and finally of Freud and the psychoanalytic movement. I first became aware of the extent of the movement prior to 1918 when I read the progress report for the years 1914–19 that appeared in the 1921 supplement to the *Internationale Zeitschrift für Psychoanalyse*. The development of the movement had various aspects: the use of psychoanalysis as therapy, the application of analytic knowledge in other scientific fields, and the training of practicing analysts.

I must emphasize here that I do not intend to embark on a short history of psychoanalysis, but will restrict myself to the part of it that was closely connected with my own life and work.

From reading Freud's first analytical writings, I sensed what the future was to confirm. But I felt no need then to know him personally, nor did I listen to the gossip concerning him, though that became almost unavoidable. There was, for instance, the pediatrician Albert Moll, whose derogatory attacks were familiar to me. There was the satirist Karl Kraus, who called psycho-analysis "that sickness which pretends to be therapy." There also appeared in Vienna's intellectual circles the gifted, schizophrenic Otto Weininger, who spoke of "the bisexuality of every cell in the human body," creating the impression that Freud's discoveries related to human bisexuality were not original. And as I have said, I heard sarcastic comments about Freud now and then at the clinic (p. 110). But in my circle of professional friends Freud was also spoken of with great interest, respect, and even with a sense of fascination.

As I absorbed Freud's teachings on the unconscious mind and began to believe in infantile sexuality and to understand fully the role of these forces in the formation of neuroses, I gradually became a devoted disciple. My position at the clinic gave me access to Freud's lectures. I appeared as a kind of hostess in a white lab coat, though I did not take any part in the proceedings. At this point I knew I was witnessing "greatness." I was not yet able to define it as Freud's genius.

My personal relationship with Freud began in August 1918. I had begun to feel restless at the clinic, and when I learned from a woman colleague that Freud had accepted her for analy-sis, I made an appointment to inquire about the possibility of a didactic analysis for myself. I arrived at the arranged time and was received by Paula, his factotum, later well known in analytic circles (she accompanied the family to England). In my talk with her I discovered that Freud's wife had pneumonia and was suffer-ing because of the severe milk shortage that still existed in Vienna. Here the two blessed goats entered the march of events; from then on, their milk was shared between my son and the Professor's wife.[1]

---

1. At about this time one of Freud's analysands, an Englishman, asked Freud to recommend a good internist for the officers of the English occupation forces. Freud gave him the name of my husband, for whose medical compe-tence he had the highest respect. Felix's new position had a very good effect on our larder: we now had not only our share of the goats' milk but also

In the course of my first interview with Freud, he asked me, "What would you do if I sent you to someone else?" to which I naturally replied, "I would not go." Freud accepted me as a patient, but with the warning that it would certainly bring me into conflict with the Wagner-Jauregg Clinic because of Wagner-Jauregg's notorious opposition to psychoanalysis. And a conflict it was indeed. Leaving the clinic meant giving up numerous advantages as a staff member, not to mention practically giving up all contact with mentally ill patients. But I did it!

From this point on, my personal destiny was closely bound up with Freud and the psychoanalytic movement. My memoirs change in character: a new chapter opens up in which all is progress, and in a new direction. I continued to live within the strong emotional unity created by my husband, my child, and myself. But Freud became the center of my intellectual sphere.

Psychoanalysis was my last and most deeply experienced revolution; and Freud, who was rightly considered a conservative on social and political issues, became for me the greatest revolutionary of the century. Looking back, I see three distinct upheavals in my life: liberation from the tyranny of my mother; the revelation of socialism; and my release from the chains of the unconscious through psychoanalysis. In each of these revolutions I was inspired and aided by a man—my father, Herman Lieberman (previously referred to as L.), and lastly Freud. My husband had his own unique place in my heart and my existence.

At the outset my analysis with Freud was not dramatic. I must admit that it is difficult to develop a normal transference neurosis with an analyst who already occupies an important position in one's psychic world. The unusual, let us say unorthodox, aspect (in opposition to the technical rules later set up at the training institutes) was that my analysis began with a certain personal relationship to Freud (the donation of the milk, for instance). This

---

the canned rations that were distributed to the English officers and their employees. We were certainly better off than most of our friends—quite a few of whom discovered in this period a renewed affection for us.

relationship not only acted as an *agent provocateur* in the first stage of analysis, but also influenced many situations during and after analysis.

Naturally I have the typical amnesic gaps that often develop after treatment, whether or not the analysis has been successful. Only isolated incidents have survived in my memory. I can recall one of the dreams I had during this period, in which I have a masculine and a feminine organ. Only later did I find out its full significance. Freud told me only that it indicated my desire to be both a boy and a girl. It was only after my analysis that it became clear to me how much my whole personality was determined by the childhood wish to be simultaneously my father's prettiest daughter and cleverest son.

From the beginning, the Oedipus complex and the feminine castration complex typically predominated over the material of my analysis. As an illustration of the former: one day I left my hour's session in a state of emotional turmoil and remained standing for a long time in front of the display window of a men's clothing store on the corner of the Berggasse. To this day I can remember each item in the display, especially the green shirts. I was weeping bitterly as I thought, "What will the Professor's poor wife do now?" for I was convinced that my analyst was in love with me and about to leave his wife, which I didn't want at all. It was a primitive Oedipal fantasy of the kind that usually develops after a certain period of analysis, when material connected with transference emerges into consciousness. I already knew about this sort of fantasy in theory, but that did not prevent me from feeling its impact in my own analysis. In my case, transference was closely related to the problems of the Oedipus complex. In fact the whole transference situation could have come out of a textbook on psychoanalysis. (By a remarkable coincidence, my father left Vienna to go home to Poland at the end of the war on the very same day in August 1918 that I began analysis with Freud.)

At that time, my son was nineteen months old. His nurse

Paula was with our family during the whole period of my analysis. She played an important role, but I do not think I spoke much about her during analytic sessions. My analysis was a didactic one, and thus a part of my professional training. I think that this feature allowed me to give in to my natural resistance and avoid mentioning conflicts with my motherhood, which included Paula. After all it was my silent agreement with this woman that made my professional activity possible: I could work on the condition that in effect I abdicate my role of mother in her favor.

My analysis ended rather abruptly about a year later, when Freud said to me with absolute candor that he needed my hour for the "Wolf-Man," [1] who, after an interruption, had come back to continue his analysis. Freud told me, "You do not need any more; you are not neurotic." I knew of this patient and realized that he was the source of important discoveries for psychoanalysis. I considered myself mature enough then to react to the situation objectively, without bringing my transference problems to bear on it. Certainly it would have been irrational for me to expect Freud to give up for my sake the time he needed for his creative work.

Nevertheless, perhaps from a feeling of rejection, I reacted by having the first depression of my life. It was a good lesson for a future analyst. Until then it had been difficult for me to comprehend the depressions of patients who had no "real causes" for such feelings.[2] The termination of my analysis wasn't a "real" cause for depression since Freud's assurance that I had no neurosis was very encouraging, and besides he had said to me, "You will now be my assistant." He added that it would not conflict with my womanhood if I continued as before in the pursuit of

1. In addition to Freud's writings on this case, the reader is referred to the Wolf-Man's recently published autobiography: *The Wolf-Man*, edited by Muriel Gardiner (New York: Basic Books, 1971).
2. I remember Freud telling a group of pupils about two of his patients who were suffering from depression: one (so she told Freud) because she was overburdened with work; the other because she "had nothing to do all day."

professional and scientific goals, thus sustaining my old identification with my father.

The honor of being chosen by Freud as his assistant cul-
minated in my participation in the sixth Congress of the International Psycho-Analytical Association in the Hague in 1920.
Karl Abraham's paper "Manifestations of the Feminine Castration Complex" impressed me all the more because Freud had
not perceived this complex in me in spite of the dream in which
I had a double set of genitals. Such reminiscences are extremely
interesting if one compares the material emerging in analysis
with insights gained long after analysis has been terminated.

The scientific knowledge I gained at the Congress and personal
meetings with many well-known analysts made it an occasion
of great significance for me. I might add that those of us from
Vienna who had gone through a period of wartime hunger appreciated the luxury of eating once again. The Dutch group of
psychoanalysts took their hungry Viennese colleagues under their
protection as soon as they guessed we might have difficulty pay-
ing our hotel bills. They invited us to stay as guests in their
homes, where they treated us to extraordinarily sumptuous
meals.

Though Freud's personality and my personal relationship with
him were of the greatest importance to me, I was motivated by
professional goals when I went to him not only as a patient but
also as a candidate. He was the creator of psychoanalysis as a
science and as a therapeutic method; since I was a future analyst
the development of this method was of major concern to me.
Thus it was both my emotional tie to Freud and my objective
realization of the need for an organized method of psychoanalytic
training that later made me very active in the field of organization.

I had become a member of the Vienna Psycho-Analytic Society
in 1918. Since there were as yet no training institutes with rigid
disciplines and sets of rules, I simply continued to work with the
patients I had begun to treat during my own analysis with Freud,

and soon established a thriving analytic practice. It was obvious that Freud had complete faith in my abilities. One proof of that was the fact that my first analytic case was a member of his family, and that he entrusted to me the complicated case of the very disturbed Victor Tausk, as well as other patients of special interest.

One of these was a young girl, the niece of one of his patients. That case brought me information that was of interest to Freud also. The girl suspected that her uncle, to whom she was engaged, was not really her uncle but her father. The uncle, who was being treated by Freud, had actually once had a relationship with the girl's mother. The aversion that my patient felt whenever her fiancé approached her sexually was the expression of her horror that these might be the sexual advances of her own father. Naturally the marriage did not take place, as Freud mentioned in an article he wrote on the case.

At this time, when training in psychoanalysis was not yet organized, control analyses were just beginning to become obligatory. My own control was with Freud. Thus he was simultaneously my training analyst and my control analyst. To be sure, this control was conducted in a very untypical way: usually our discussions were prefaced by Freud's modest remark, "You know more about the patient than I do, because you see him every day; I can't tell you very much—but then, you don't need it anyway." However, when I specifically asked him for advice, he was always willing to give it. He continued to show an interest in the cases he had sent to me, and I requested consultations when special difficulties arose. But such conferences gradually grew less frequent. My later professional conferences with Freud were less directly didactic. They were real discussions, partly theoretical and partly clinical in nature.

I pass now from my personal contact with Freud to memories of the Psycho-Analytic Society. At the time when I became a member, in 1918, Alfred Adler and Wilhelm Stekel were no longer there. Nor was Jung, but this was of lesser significance for the Vienna group. Otto Rank was still active as Freud's favorite disciple; later I witnessed the break between them, which was obviously very painful for Freud.

Hermine von Hug-Hellmuth was the only other woman member I found at the roundtable meetings the Psycho-Analytic Society held every Wednesday evening. She was a small woman with black hair, always neatly, one might even say ascetically, dressed. Her former profession of teaching had left a certain mark on her.

She was the editor of the *Tagebuch Eines Halbwüchsigen Mädchens* (*Diary of an Adolescent Girl*), which gives us a classic picture of feminine adolescence. People said that this diary was a creation of her fantasy, to which I would answer that if this was the case, Dr. Hug-Hellmuth had both psychological insight and literary talent. The Society's skepticism went to such an extreme that one of our leading members played detective and inquired in all the hospitals whether a man of a certain description had been admitted on the date when the diarist of the *Tagebuch* reports that her father fell ill. His inquiries achieved only negative results. Then, as now, such facts were immaterial; the book is so true psychologically that it has become a gem of psychoanalytic literature.

Unfortunately the quiet, withdrawn Dr. Hug-Hellmuth herself became the real-life heroine of an even greater drama than the one in the *Diary*. She had never married nor had children, but her longing for motherhood was fulfilled when she adopted a small boy, reportedly the illegitimate child of her sister—at any rate she referred to him as "my nephew" in her writings and lectures. When this boy reached adolescence, he murdered his aunt, who had taken care of him for so long and given him a home. Apparently it happened when she refused to give him a sum of money he had asked her for. At the trial the young man said that he had always been to her merely a guinea pig for her psychological experiments. Perhaps this was true, for she was indeed completely engrossed in theoretical learning, and tried to use her personal experiences in furthering her scientific pursuits.

The young man was released from prison after serving his sentence for murder. The first thing he did was to turn to an old psychoanalyst friend of his aunt for financial help and therapy. The analyst was of the opinion that a woman analyst would be best—she could in effect replace the deceased aunt! He suggested me. My husband and I, both aware of the danger that I might become the aunt's substitute as a target, were opposed to this suggestion. The nephew did not come to me for analysis, but soon my husband became aware of a figure lurking around our house that corresponded to descriptions he had heard of the young ex-convict. In order not to alarm me, my husband told me nothing of this. But I began to notice that the same young man would be walking some distance behind me on my solitary walks in the park near our house. Later I noticed another young man in the distance, also walking alone. The first was the nephew, the other a private detective hired by Felix to protect me. I don't know what eventually became of the nephew, but he seems not to have committed any further crimes.

This incident brings to mind a truth well known to any child psychologist: children want to be loved, not observed. Poor Dr. Hug-Hellmuth became a victim of her own approach to child psychology.

In my reminiscences about the women who played a part in the psychoanalytic movement, I am limiting myself to those with who I came into direct contact. Some of them were older than I professionally—that is, they belonged to a slightly earlier period of the movement. Several happened to be Polish, and perhaps for this reason were of special interest to me. There was G. Sokolnicka, for instance, who appears in Gide's autobiographical novel *The Counterfeiters*. In real life, she was Gide's analyst when he was seventeen years old. Another colleague was my dear friend Mira Oberholzer, who remained true to Freud until her death, despite the developments in Switzerland, where Jung eventually "won out" over Freud.

Three of Freud's women pupils achieved a certain degree of prominence as "pioneers in feminine psychology" (that was the phrase Freud used in his writings). These were Ruth Mack-Brunswick, Jeanne Lampl-de Groot, and myself. I experienced this linking of my name with two other women's as a kind of trauma. It seemed to be a repetition of my childhood, when I was one of three sisters—though in the later trio I was not the youngest. But now I was a mature woman and had the opportunity to deal with this problem in analysis. Whether it was because of my analysis with Freud or my knowledge of his respect for me, I eventually lost my feelings of competition and jealousy. These feelings never recurred during my later career. I was too fascinated with the work and too aware of my increasingly secure place in the psychoanalytic movement to become involved in rivalries.

I cannot move on into the next section of my autobiography without mentioning Marie Bonaparte, that unusual figure in the history of psychoanalysis. I think that of all the more or less famous women who appeared during the last period of Freud's work in Vienna, she played a unique and most important role. She was an ardent disciple, admirer, and friend of Freud—and it was she who in the moment of crisis took him and his books, notes, and collections out of Nazi-occupied Vienna and thus probably saved his life. She wrote an autobiography, especially interesting for its description of her childhood, which, since she was born into the richest line of the Bonapartes, was surrounded with regal pomp and splendor. She liked to tell us—a small circle of her new professional friends—fascinating stories of her life, in which the great wealth and glory of Napoleon and his descendants played an important role. She evidently had a lonely childhood, and perhaps this was one of the reasons that her great intellectual curiosity dominated her life from a very early age.

I do not know what brought her to Freud; probably it was her neurotic needs. From the beginning of my acquaintance with her, I was struck by her immense erudition in many fields. Her scientific contributions to psychoanalysis were solid but for me personally not exciting. But conversations with her revealed the great variety of her interests, stimulated and influenced by the circle of prominent scientists surrounding her in her youth. Her three-volume biography of Edgar Allan Poe as well as her publications on mythology and anthropology have always shown solid knowledge of her subject.

Our mutual interest in female masochism brought us together, and a humorous misunderstanding contributed to our relationship: she was notified by a friend that H.D.[1] had died unexpectedly. Marie, misled by the identical initials, wrote a letter of condolence to Felix which by its beauty and sincerity became a significant memento for me.

What impressed me most about her was her fanatic dedication to justice, which caused her to fight with all her strength for relatively small goals. Nothing was too small for her attention when it related to injustice suffered by a human being. For example, she made the long journey from Greece to America in order to attempt to reverse the death sentence of Caryl Chessman; his autobiographical description of his punishment for the seduction of young girls convinced her that he was the victim of an unjust application of the law. She hired the best lawyers, but was unsuccessful in her attempts. For this and similar actions Lucie Jessner, a great admirer of hers, was to call her laughingly "the madwoman of Chaillot." For years I stayed in correspondence with her and met her occasionally at international psychoanalytic conferences; I was very grieved by her sudden death in 1962. This abbreviated description of her has been adapted to the scale of my short autobiography, but I suppose that the literature on her in various languages is extensive.

I did my work under the aegis of the Vienna Psycho-Analytic Society, and was proud of having a place at its roundtable discussions, presided over by Freud during this still loosely organized, creative period of the movement. Acceptance into the Society involved one formality: every prospective member had to

1. Hilda Doolittle.

read a paper, on the basis of which he was either accepted or rejected. The topic assigned to me was "A Critical Review of Lou Salome's Article *Vaginal and Anal.*" This article was unnecessary, speculative, hard to comprehend, and completely alien to my own psychological thinking. Perhaps the antipathy I felt from the beginning for this highly gifted woman stemmed from the labor her article cost me.

I didn't have an easy time at the start of my career in the Society. My next lecture was on the psychosomatic changes my sister Malvina's younger son underwent after the death of his older brother (see p. 60). It was received with skepticism, and Freud at first said of it: "If it weren't Dr. Helene Deutsch who is telling us this story, we wouldn't believe it." To me this meant, "It isn't true." And yet it was! Eventually I did manage to convince Freud of the story's accuracy; his beautiful explanation of it has already been quoted in a previous chapter.

Anna Freud's paper "Beating Phantasies and Day Dreams" resulted in her acceptance into the Society in 1922. Her talent was evident even then. When I expressed my good opinion of this lecture to Freud, he broke into the typical smile of a proud father. What struck me especially about this lecture was that she spoke from memory without any notes. The same held true for all her later talks, which bore so clearly the mark of her great father.

Anna Freud was a devoted teacher of young children, and her development towards child analysis was based on her teaching experience. She started her work with individual cases of disturbed children as a continuation of her previous work with normal children and developed techniques of treatment that became fundamental in child analysis. Freud once said about the process of identification in melancholia: "The shadow of the object falls on the psychic life of an individual." About Anna Freud one can say that the light of her father fell on her professional work and changed a talented teacher into a creative child analyst. At the beginning of her career she was often the target of attacks from the enemies of psychoanalysis, as her father had been. However, Anna persevered in her work. The clarity of her thinking and her emphasis on direct experience enabled her to develop a successful approach to the treatment of disturbed children that was to win her many pupils. Of the pupils who worked with Anna in Vienna, the most outstanding ones were Marianne Kris, Anny Angel-Katan, and Jenny Wälder-Hall. Over the years they themselves have become leaders in the field.

Anna Freud was not the only leader in the new field of child analysis. Melanie Klein had developed a different approach in her work and aroused great interest in her speculative theories, especially in England. Ernest Jones was one of her chief supporters. My personal contact with Melanie Klein was quite active in the period when both of us were analysands of Karl Abraham in Berlin. I think that Abraham achieved therapeutic success in treating Mrs. Klein's neurotic problems, but her analysis did not have a lasting influence on her extremely speculative thinking in child analysis. I was often a listener to her speculations, since during our analysis we lived in the same *pension* near Abraham's office.

Anna Freud remains a leader in child analysis, and most of the important figures in the field have worked with her either in Vienna or in England. After Freud and his family escaped to London in 1938, Anna founded there the now-famous Hampstead Clinic, where she continues to treat children and to teach child analysis. Many of the best child analysts of the younger generation have learned their profession there with Anna or under the aegis of Anna's pupils. Experience with child analysis is not yet an obligatory part of psychoanalytic training, but I assume that the next International Psycho-Analytic Congress will bring us closer to that aim.

My own experience was very largely with adolescents and adults, so childhood was a *terra incognita* to me until the birth of my own son. It was too late for me to become a pupil of Anna

Freud, but I shared with others a great respect for her work, increased by my dedication to Freud and my awareness of his own respect for "Antigone"—the name he gave to his illustrious daughter.

Anna's work was not exclusively with children; she moved very quickly also into the area of adult analysis and, above all, training analysis. She soon became one of the most sought-after training analysts, and quite a number of the younger generation's outstanding analysts were her analysands. Her publications are among the most widely read and quoted works in psychoanalytic literature.

We worked together in the Vienna Institute, and there were never any serious elements of controversy between us. Like me, Anna was the youngest of three sisters and her father's chosen heir, the one sharing her father's interests and strivings. This might have been a reason for the ease with which I often identified with her. We had first met in the Wagner-Jauregg Clinic when I was a staff member and Anna was attending Freud's lectures there; I still remember how she looked entering the lecture hall on the arm of her father. When we reminisce about our first meeting Anna can visualize my white doctor's coat and I recall that she wore a green suit on that occasion. From the beginning I felt a kind of tenderness toward her that never left me, notwithstanding her eventual fame and importance in the psychoanalytic movement. From time to time Felix (also a devoted friend of Anna's) and I would visit "Hochroterd," Anna's little farm near Vienna, where she enjoyed a modest kind of farming. The Sundays we spent with her are perhaps even clearer in my memory than our work in the service of psychoanalysis. For my husband and me, "Hochroterd" was the seed of our love for our own American farm, "Babayaga."

I think that my great joy in Anna's success and my admiration for her work and her talent as a speaker are a continuation of our closeness in Vienna. On very special occasions I still wear a black blouse Anna knitted for me in the early days of our friendship. There were years of separation in which I was preoccupied with my own problems, but my husband never forgot to send flowers to Anna each Christmas.

During a vacation in London in recent years, I visited Anna at the Hampstead Clinic, and was enchanted by the harmonious atmosphere that prevailed and by the devotion of her co-workers. I participated in one of the staff meetings, at which the topic under discussion was heroic acts carried out by children, that is, rescuing other children from water, fire, etc., thereby endangering their own lives. The group discussed how difficult it is to get these children into analysis and how little they make of their own heroic actions. Requested to participate in the discussion, I declared that since I had not had much experience with children, I would offer instead a true story from my own childhood: during one of my visits to my cousins in Stryj, a heavy rain changed the harmless little local river into a dangerous rapid torrent. We children were strictly forbidden to go swimming. As we were standing disappointed on the bank, we suddenly caught sight of a little boy, less cautious than we, who had tried to go swimming and was now helplessly being carried downstream. I was an excellent swimmer and had always had the feeling that no accident could ever happen to me in the water. Without hesitation I jumped into the current and rescued the young boy. In the little town of Stryj news of my exploit traveled quickly, and for a short time I was the heroine of the hour. In the ensuing discussion, Anna asked me what I had found out about my motivation for this act in my analysis with Freud. To this I answered, "Oh, I never mentioned it in my analysis." Anna recalls that this impressed everyone enormously since it fitted in so well with what they had found out about these heroic children.

But now I am getting ahead of myself, and I would like to return to my more or less chronological narrative.

Of Freud's men pupils who were of personal importance to me I would set Karl Abraham at the head of the list. In later years he became my analyst and a warm friendship formed a bond between us until his death. Not long ago I found an old letter from him, in which he writes that he has just visited Freud and that Freud on that occasion spoke of me with great warmth and affection.

Abraham's Don Quixote side was not obvious to Freud at the beginning, for he kept his warm personality and rich imagination hidden behind a sober façade. But gradually he became one of Freud's most respected pupils. His relatively early death was a great blow to me personally and to the psychoanalytic movement. Freud said of Abraham, in the only funeral eulogy he ever wrote:

> With this man—*integer vitae scelerisque purus*—we are burying one of the brightest hopes of our young science which is still facing so many attacks—perhaps an irreplaceable part of its future. Among all those who have followed me on the dark paths of psychoanalytic work, he won so prominent a place that only one other name could be placed next to his. The trust of his colleagues and students, which he possessed to an unlimited degree, would surely have called him to a position of leadership, and undoubtedly he would have been an exemplary leader in the search for truth, not led astray by the praise or disapproval of the crowd, nor by the alluring light of any fantasy images of his own.[1]

I assume that the "other name" Freud refers to was that of Sandor Ferenczi, whom he had designated to come from Budapest to lead the Vienna psychoanalytic group after Freud's retirement because of his illness.

It was Abraham, a keen observer, who first detected in Otto Rank's peculiar activities in America a danger to the psychoanalytic movement. Freud's relationship with Rank was at first characterized by great respect and confidence. The deep causes of their eventual split cannot be explained away simply by the fact that this was a typical and often repeated pattern in Freud's life. I believe that for every extremely gifted person who has fantasized about being a genius—and most gifted people have—submission to a real genius contains an element of tragedy. This seemed to be true in Rank's case.

1. *Internationale Zeitschrift fur Psychoanalyse,* vol. xii, part 1, 1926.

We could see that Rank was already deeply entangled in this tragic situation when he made his first visit to America. I was perhaps somewhat better acquainted with the problem than the others, because I had been a friend of his first wife, Beata, almost from the beginning of their marriage. Beata Rank was an intelligent young girl who was working as a secretary in Kraków during World War I. Through her work she met Otto, stationed there as an officer in the army. They were married and he brought her back to his small two-room apartment in Vienna, where they lived a simple but obviously contented life. After a year they had a child, who later made friends with my three-year-old Martin in the public park near our home. In this way I came to know Beata without being aware of her husband's professional identity. We were both Polish and both very interested in our small children. What happened later on in the psyche of this small, quiet woman that changed her whole personality? This I do not know.

In Vienna, she came to know Anna Freud and joined her in her work at the Internationaler Psychoanalytischer Verlag. When she left for America, she and Otto were already divorced and he was married to an American. At first she had difficulties in establishing analytic practice in Boston because of her lay status, but William Healy and Augusta Bronner gave her a position at the Judge Baker Foundation. Here, instead of becoming active in social work, as we had expected, she stayed in psychoanalysis, remaining loyal to Freud in her approach. She had a very successful career as a lay analyst, eventually even becoming an active training analyst. Her most important work was with the "atypical" children at the James Jackson Putnam Children's Center. She has contributed extensively to our understanding of such children.

Beata Rank was extremely gifted in her work, but a certain weakness in her personality structure caused psychological problems. Probably I ought to substitute the term "neurosis" for "weakness." Although she was loved and admired by many, she suffered from a painful though unjustified sense of inferiority.

To return to Otto Rank: in America a greed for money, completely alien to his character until then, seems to have developed in him. After his return he moved from Vienna to Paris, to a palatial residence in the Bois de Boulogne, where his wife maintained a luxurious salon frequented by many celebrated artists. Patronage on this scale was expensive; consequently Rank had to keep up his contact with America in order to retain this source of income. By this time, he was no longer working within the framework of Freud's teachings.

During Freud's illness and first operation for cancer Otto Rank was not in Vienna, but I suspect that the depression he felt then, in America, was an act of mourning connected with Freud's illness. Perhaps he felt in this period that he was the successor to the throne and the fact that Freud survived the operation and continued to work was a disappointment to him. He introduced a new theory concerning the "trauma of birth" into psychoanalysis, ignoring the fact that Freud had already treated this subject, relating the anxiety-free nature of Macduff in *Macbeth* to the circumstance of his birth by Caesarean section.

Initially Freud did not oppose Rank's theory, but eventually he came to reject it as a plagiarism. He especially objected to Rank's exaggeration of the importance of the "trauma of birth" in the etiology of neurosis. Freud always gave freely to his pupils, but was very sensitive about having his ideas taken away. He had gone through this before, with Adler and Jung.

In speaking of Viennese analysts I cannot omit Theodor Reik, whom Freud supported as a practicing therapist largely because Reik seemed to be a victim of the Vienna medical establishment's ostracism. The official policy was that the treatment of mentally disturbed patients was the exclusive right of the medical profession, and Reik was accused of malpractice. This was a signal to Freud to send patients to Reik. Only the intervention of the influential Professor Tandler, at Freud's request, helped Reik out of this ominous situation. I must say that without any prejudice against lay analysis on my side, I had no confidence in

Reik as a therapist. He simply was not interested in neurotic illness. (In this respect he was not unlike Hanns Sachs.) Various cases that came to my attention made it clear to me that Reik was much more interested in Anatole France and in problems of the psychology of religion than he was in the fate of his patients. When he published his book *Listening with the Third Ear* about his experience as an analyst, I remember thinking, "He must have had the other two shut." But I must emphasize that these remarks refer only to Reik's activities in Vienna; it is possible that his later work in America underwent changes of which I am ignorant.

I would also like to mention another lay analyst, Abram Kardiner, a writer of outstanding books in the field of anthropology, whose dignity and erudition inspired in me an automatic confidence in his work. His book on the Marquesas culture [1] proved invaluable to me in my work on motherhood in the second volume of *The Psychology of Women*.

1. *The Individual and His Society: The Psychodynamics of Primitive Social Organization* (New York: Columbia University Press, 1939).

XI

Research and Teaching in Vienna

I MUST REPEAT that this period of direct contact with Freud was a stimulating, joyous time for me—I was sitting at the same table with Freud at the meetings of the Vienna Psycho-Analytic Society. Freud, the Society's chairman, was then performing the function later taken over by the Training Institute: the selection of new members on the basis of personal and professional qualifications and of the lecture given by the prospective member. In fact it was always Freud's personal opinion that was decisive. Shortly after I was accepted into the Society, I entered a creative phase; I had many ideas and began to attract attention in analytic circles. Some of my papers were clinical and some were on the application of psychoanalysis to non-medical fields. Many of them were concerned with the problems of women. My intense interest in women stemmed from various sources: first, from my own narcissism, a wish to know myself; second, from the fact that research until then had been chiefly concerned with men. Later on a third motive was added: Freud's interest in feminine psychology, which made me want to answer his questions in this field through my own investigations and so to reverse his dictum, "Woman does not betray her secret."

I made the problems of feminine sexuality my chief subject of study, and the first courses I offered at the Society were almost exclusively concerned with them. Characteristically I soon grew bored with these courses and gave them over to my younger colleagues Grete Bibring and Jeanne de Groot (not yet Lampl at the time). My lecture series "The Psychoanalytic Study of Neurosis" also seems to have been useful in those early days of analytic education. I laid no claim to theoretical originality, and generally relied on Freud's clinical work. Later on I had enough cases in my own practice to use them, with discretion, for purposes of instruction.

When I look over my publications I discover a circle enclosing the greatest part of my work, starting in 1925 with *Zur Psychologie der Weiblichen Sexualfunktionen* (*On the Psychology of Sexual Functions in Women*),[1] and ending in 1945, with the two volumes of *The Psychology of Women*.[2] It is evident that the first publication already contains all the building stones for the latter. What was first conceived by intuition and observation of a small number of analyzed women was later supported and confirmed by thirty years of experience.

In the course of a long professional life I have been occupied with many diverse problems, mostly of a clinical nature. I believe that my publications have contributed something to psychoanalysis as an exploration of man's inner life. Nonetheless, *The Psychology of Women* has become a sort of label for me, and even today I am still primarily associated with it, although I have treated many other subjects that interested me more. Once I immersed myself for weeks in a study of Don Quixote and received my reward in Freud's interest in my work. I learned only later that his personal sympathy was always with the "Fool," the person not too closely attached to reality. This fact helps explain

1. Vienna: Internationaler Psychoanalytischer Verlag, 1925.
2. New York: Grune & Stratton, 1944.

Freud's great interest in the therapeutic ideas of Dr. Georg Grod-deck, which were taken seriously by only a few, among them Sandor Ferenczi.

It often happened that a fresh interest of mine, seemingly independent of Freud in its origins, actually came to life at his instigation, however indirect the stimulus may have been. Thus I became interested at one time in the problems of plagiarism, only to learn much later that these had once weighed very heavily on Freud. This occurred when his close friend Wilhelm Fliess was struggling to convince the others that he, and not Freud, was the first to consider the problem of bisexuality and its relationship to neurotic illness. My awareness of this incident had been very vague, yet evidently it was enough to stimulate me to do a study of plagiarism later on. Years afterward, I became fascinated with Dionysus; I have the feeling that I found out about Freud's interest in that figure, consciously at least, only after I had written my book *A Psychoanalytic Study of the Myth of Dionysus and Apollo.*[1] My own study brought out the fact that Dionysus was engaged in a continual battle for his seat on Olympus during the whole of his mythical existence. Freud had limited himself to the assertion that Dionysus was never a god.

It was Dionysus who first turned my interest from contemporary problems to a study of classical antiquity; but even here my interest centered on themes that had already been of special interest to me in the past: motherhood and the mother-son relationship. In this book I used mythological figures to represent two contrasting relationships of a son to his mother: Apollo, the son who kills the mother; and Dionysus, the son who saves her.

Freud's lifelong interest in literature, especially the Greek classics, is evidenced by penetrating comments scattered through-

1. New York: International Universities Press, 1969. I had the honor of reading this essay before the New York Psychoanalytic Institute on Freud's birthday, May 6, 1967, as that year's Freud Anniversary Lecture.

out his writings, as well as by his psychoanalytical interpretations of figures in literature. An early description of an anxiety dream, for example, occurred in his aforementioned analysis of Wilhelm Jensen's novel *Gradiva*.[1]

It is not surprising that poetry and mythology should have served Freud as a treasury of source material. Psychoanalysis has from the beginning been a borderline discipline between the humanities and the natural sciences. Freud oscillated between these two aspects during his whole life. In his works he managed to combine the knowledge of a scientist with the insight and often the style of a poet. Although Freud never won the Nobel Prize, which he deserved, he was awarded the Goethe Prize in 1930 in recognition of his literary achievements.

In an unpublished paper, Richard Sterba has pointed out that Freud's whole approach to psychoanalysis was shaped by the tradition of classical humanism he imbibed as a *Gymnasiast*. This type of education was primarily literary, with stress on Greek and Latin, as opposed to the more scientific curriculum of the *Realschule*.

His belief in the value of classical culture pervades his writings throughout his life. This humanistic order in which he had been raised remained for him the Kybernetes, the guide of behavior, and provided for him the aims in life and the values in which he believed. . . . Freud's psychological interest, though it seems to have grown out of his neurological studies, was generated primarily by his appreciation of and respect for human feelings. This attitude toward feelings without which all his psychodynamic discoveries could not have been possible was the result of his human as well as his humanistic interest in the emotions of other people, an attitude to which the knowledge of the great literature of the ancient classics contributed as much as did the world-literature of the more modern times and cultures.[1]

Like most of the older generation of European psychoanalysts, I too was educated in this classical tradition, though stimulated

1. "The Psychoanalyst in a World of Change" (Herman Nunberg Lecture, delivered to the New York Academy of Medicine, April 2, 1968).

by modern European literature as well. Many of my psycho-analytic articles have been on literary topics (George Sand, *Lord Jim, Don Quixote,* etc.)

I based one of my papers [1] on Balzac's *Deux Femmes,* a novel that is a perceptive study of the complementary psychology of two women. The motherly woman in this novel, who is wholly devoted to her child, is full of secret cravings for erotic adventure. The other woman, experienced in love, longs to have a child. In our present society we can see many examples of Balzac's two women in modern attire: sociological changes have merely given these psychological facts slightly modified forms of expression. Balzac's fascinating study illustrates clearly the writer's ability to comprehend, by means of his art, the inner springs of human emotions and behavior.

The close kinship between literature and psychoanalysis was borne out for me once more when I discovered the clear resemblance between Chekhov's story "Dushenka" ("The Darling") and a paper of mine dealing with the pathology of emotions. The paper is a discussion of an emotionally distorted type of human being who can sustain his own personality only through identification with others (the "as if" personality). The heroine of Chekhov's story cannot love someone without adopting his opinions and interests, down to the last detail.

Neither she nor the veterinary surgeon said anything to anyone about the change in their relationship. They tried to conceal it, but without success, for Olga could not keep a secret. When she handed round tea or served supper to his visitors, fellow-officers of his regiment, she would begin talking about foot-and-mouth disease or tuberculosis among the cattle, or about the municipal slaughter-houses, while he looked terribly embarrassed; and after the visitors had gone he would seize her by the arm and hiss angrily:

"I've told you a hundred times not to talk about something you don't understand. When we vets are talking among ourselves, please don't interfere. Why, it's just silly!"

1. "Motherhood and Sexuality," *Psychoanalytic Quarterly,* 2:476–488; also in *Neuroses and Character Types* (New York: International Universities Press, 1965), pp. 190–202.

She would look at him with astonishment. "But what am I to talk about, darling?" she would ask him is dismay.[1]

Thus the essential characteristic of the person I wish to describe is that outwardly he conducts his life as if he possessed a complete and sensitive emotional capacity. To him there is no difference between his empty forms and what others actually experience. Without going deeper into the matter I wish at this point to state that this condition is not identical with the coldness of repressed individuals in whom there is usually a highly differentiated emotional life hidden behind a wall, the loss of affect being either manifest or cloaked by overcompensations. . . . The apparently normal relationship to the world corresponds to a child's imitativeness and is the expression of identification with the environment, a mimicry which results in an ostensibly good adaptation to the world of reality despite the absence of object cathexis.

Further consequences of such a relationship to life are a completely passive attitude to the environment with a highly plastic readiness to pick up signals from the outer world and to mold oneself and one's behavior accordingly. The identification with what other people are thinking and feeling, is the expression of this passive plasticity and renders the person capable of the greatest fidelity and the basest perfidy. Any object will do as a bridge for identification. At first the love, friendship, and attachment of an "as if" person have something very rewarding for the partner. If it is a woman, she seems to be the quintessence of feminine devotion, an impression which is particularly imparted by her passivity and readiness for identification. Soon, however, the lack of real warmth brings such an emptiness and dullness to the emotional atmosphere that the man as a rule precipitously breaks off the relationship. In spite of the adhesiveness which the "as if" person brings to every relationship, when he is thus abandoned he displays either a rush of affective reactions which are "as if" and thus spurious, or a frank absence of affectivity. At the very first opportunity the former object is exchanged for a new one and the process is repeated.[2]

I did not know about Dushenka when I was writing my paper on the "as if" personality.[3] Chekhov was a physician and psy-

1. *Lady with Lapdog, and Other Stories,* trans. David Magarshack (Harmondsworth, Middlesex, England: Penguin Books Ltd, 1964), p. 258.
2. "Some Forms of Emotional Disturbance and Their Relationship to Schizophrenia" *Psychoanalytic Quarterly* 11:303–305; also in *Neuroses and Character Types* (New York: International Universities Press, 1965).
3. I might add here that Freud alerted me to the fact that the original title of my paper, "Als Ob," had been used before by the German philosopher

chiatrist by profession, but his understanding of the human soul had its roots in a deeper faculty, his poetic imagination.

Another example of literary illustration occurs to me with regard to one of Freud's papers. Some of his observations on the psychological events in melancholia are contained in his article "Mourning and Melancholia" (1915). I discovered a remarkable analogy in Flaubert's description of Charles Bovary's grief after his wife's death—a grief Charles expresses by consciously adopting his dead wife's personality and habits.

To please her, as if she were still living, he adopted her taste, her ideas; he bought patent leather boots and took to wearing white cravats. He waxed his moustache and, just like her, signed promissory notes. She corrupted him from beyond the grave.

He was obliged to sell his silver piece by piece; next he sold the drawing-room furniture. All the rooms were stripped; but the bedroom, her own room, remained as before. After his dinner Charles went up there. He pushed the round table in front of the fire and drew up *her* arm-chair. He sat down facing it. A candle burnt in one of the gilt candelsticks.[1]

Freud had arrived at these insights by scientific observation; Flaubert through his poetic intuition.

If I do not refer to more modern writers, it is not because I do not appreciate their insights, but because they are not so deeply engraved on my mind as the writers I loved in my youth, when the experience of literature had an immense influence on my emotional life. (Because of the intensity of my feeling for literature, and certain specific talents she had observed in me, Aunt Frania had predicted that I would one day be a writer. This prediction did not fully materialize. But when I look over a list of my publications, I see that there was some truth in it, after all.)

Hans Vaihinger for a book of his which invested the phrase with a meaning totally different from the one I gave it. Since it was absolutely impossible for me to find a new title that could so well sum up the essence of this personality type, I simply kept the original title.

1. Gustave Flaubert, *Madame Bovary*, trans. Paul DeMan (New York: W.W. Norton & Company, 1966), p. 250.

To leave the Muses and return to the more realistic story of the Vienna psychoanalytic movement: a new chapter began in 1920 when I learned that a Polyclinic had been inaugurated in Berlin under the direction of Dr. Max Eitingon. Naturally this awakened in me the wish to have a psychiatric clinic in Vienna as a forerunner to a training institute of our own. In 1922 this wish was fulfilled and psychiatric training entered a new phase.

The Psychoanalytic Ambulatorium was established with the help of my husband Felix, who, as director of the Clinic for Heart Diseases at the University of Vienna Hospital, made the arrangements to secure an appropriate location. I remember that Felix called the Ambulatorium his birthday present to me.

Dr. Eduard Hitschmann and his assistant (later co-director) Dr. Wilhelm Reich, after heading a clinic for neurotically ill patients, took over the direction of the Ambulatorium. After the Vienna Training Institute was established three years later (1925), the Ambulatorium became the Institute's major source of control cases for candidates. My office while I was director of the Training Institute was on the Wollzeilgasse, about a half hour's walking distance from the Ambulatorium, which was on the Pelikangasse. Dr. Hitschmann once quipped, in reference to our differing diagnoses of his patients, "How odd it is that what in my opinion is a harmless case of hysteria will often develop into a case of schizophrenia by the time it reaches the Wollzeilgasse!"

The Psycho-Analytic Society, with Freud as its chairman, continued to be the focus of my interest. As long as he was present, I regarded each Wednesday evening conference as an important scientific event. Large parts of most of his publications of this period were first presented as lectures to the Society and discussed by us afterwards. The remarks he contributed to the discussions of other members' lectures were equally valuable. He could take even a minute, insignificant report by one of his pupils and with commentary make it into a wellspring of psychoanalytic insights.

But there came a time when Freud began to restrict his activities. A small group of chosen younger analysts became the beneficiaries of this change. Freud declared he was retiring, but that he wished, through the Society, to remain in contact with the progress being made in psychoanalysis. The Wednesday night meetings were now held at Freud's house at 19 Berggasse, and the number of participants was reduced to twelve—six permanent and six rotating members. Thus it became possible to give a considerable number of gifted young people of the next generation a chance to come into contact with the venerated teacher. My husband and I belonged to the group of permanent members.

Freud opened the first meeting at his house with a declaration that took us by surprise: "I have nothing more to say, and now I want to learn from you." So we brought out our small contributions, which we had actually intended to use only as cues for Freud. I was one of the first to speak. Following the wishes of the small group, I initiated a discussion on the problem of "psychic trauma." By the end of the evening it was incomprehensible to us why Freud had declared he had nothing more to say, for his remarks, as always, added significantly to our understanding of the problem under discussion.

Of the subsequent discussions, I remember the clinical ones better than the theoretical-speculative ones. The most important paper read was Robert Wälder's critique of Freud's book *Inhibition, Symptom and Anxiety* (*The Problem of Anxiety*). This paper aroused great enthusiasm in Freud. Another topic discussed was the problem of the termination of analysis, which remains with us even today. Another concerned psychic occurrences within the analyst himself; I believe that what we now call counter-transference did not yet have this name. Freud was of the opinion that the analyst has an inclination toward neurotic reactions because in his professional work he must continually suppress his own emotional impulses. Later during the discussion he expressed the idea that it might benefit the analyst to undergo a short follow-up analysis every few years (he mentioned five years as a possibility).

One thing has remained indelibly in my mind from those

evenings with Freud: every discussion was suffused with that wonderful aura of cautiousness we encounter also in Freud's writings: "If I am not mistaken. . . ." Freud's greatness was evident not only in the brilliance of his ideas but also in his objective attitude toward any topic under consideration. For the small groups that came together then at Freud's house, those intimate talks have been a source of inspiring memories. My husband and, I believe, Dr. Otto Isakower made notes on the sessions. Those of my husband seem to have shared the fate of his whole correspondence with Freud: they are preserved in the Library of Congress for future historical studies. I have no information about Isakower's records. Dr. Paul Federn also took detailed notes on these meetings, and his son Ernst together with Dr. Herman Nunberg published them in America.

Simultaneously with these events centered around Freud, the Psycho-Analytic Society was making fruitful progress but at the same time struggling against obstacles. One of these sprang from the activities, and even more from the personality, of Wilhelm Reich. His collaboration was for a time welcome and stimulating. He worked in the Ambulatorium and his clinical reports were usually very informative for his younger colleagues. After a time he himself devalued the quality of his work by trying to make certain ideas, correct in themselves, but obvious and not entirely original, into the central concept of psychoanalysis. His aggressive way of advancing these ideas was typical of him.

His premise that every analysis should begin with a discussion of negative transference stood in fundamental opposition to the analytic method of free association. At my suggestion, a seminar was organized in which one of the participants would give a chronological presentation of his case for discussion. In this way, Reich's obstinate insistence upon his ideas could be submitted to an objective control. My suggestion proved fruitful, and later became the basis of what is today called the "control seminar," in which a candidate periodically reports on one of his cases to a group of fellow analysts, who then discuss the case together.

I will not write at length about Reich's later career. His fanatical belief in the role of the orgasm as the central life force and the subsequent popularity of an expanded version of this belief are generally known. Psychoanalysts, especially Freud, very early felt estranged from Reich, not because of his political radicalism (as his followers claimed) but because his presumptuous and aggressive, I might even say paranoid, personality was hard to bear. What later became a delusion appeared at first to be a rational but fanatically overemphasized idea that interfered with his participation in the training at the Institute. His distortion of the relationship of psychoanalysis to sexuality, his false propaganda of the orgiastic "ideology" among adolescents, without any regard for the crucial process of sublimation—all these naturally provoked analysts into serious protest.

Until Freud's exile, Vienna remained the international center for psychoanalytic treatment and teaching. The term "psychoanalytic movement" is taken to mean the scientific work of Freud and his pupils, the application of analysis as a therapeutic method, and the training of future analysts. Although its practical applications in therapy and in non-medical fields have undergone modifications, what is known as "classic analysis" (Freud's pupils have never used this expression) has remained virtually the same.

In the period before the training institutes were organized, the Vienna Psycho-Analytic Society as a whole was the training organization, Freud himself being responsible for the selection and evaluation of candidates. Training then consisted of seminars in which prospective analysts were instructed, under the direction of experienced members of the Society, about the neurotic problems of patients chosen as suitable for teaching purposes. At this time Freud considered only cases of hysteria and obsessional neurosis as suitable for psychoanalytic treatment, and excluded what we now call "character neurosis" and "narcissistic neurosis."

Freud continued to be very interested in the problems of training. He always strongly emphasized the qualifications of an individual candidate as opposed to rigid official requirements. In a 1928 letter to Franz Alexander, he wrote:

I am afraid that renouncing any *preliminary* choice (of candidates) would threaten us with an excess of work that often would be useless. There is no assurance that the analysis would bring about the necessary character changes, and in any event it presupposes years of effort; you could hardly expect that to be agreed on in Vienna, for example, where almost all the training analyses are carried out *gratis*.[1]

Freud always considered the personality of the candidate more important than his formal qualifications. His dismissal of the medical degree as a condition of acceptance into the training program stems from this emphasis on character. This was also the motivation for his paper *The Question of Lay Analysis.* I too have always considered the candidate's character the most significant factor—not only because of Freud's influence but also from my own convictions. Freud felt that one must make a judgment about the candidate's capacity for becoming an analyst at the very beginning, *before* one accepted him or her for training. In the course of the years since then, the subject of lay analysis has become again and again a strongly controversial one, and I have found myself standing with divided loyalties between Freud, who held that medical study was not essential to psychoanalytic training, and my husband, who considered it a prerequisite. Between 1928 and the present day a great amount of organizational work has been done, and the problem expressed in Freud's letter to Alexander has been solved.

The generally uniform nature of psychoanalytic training in all countries arises from the fact that organizational problems were formulated and discussed at international congresses and directed by an international committee on psychoanalytic training. Before 1925 there existed special training institutes in Budapest and Berlin; these created a pattern of organization that the later Vienna Training Institute also accepted. Special international conferences worked out further developments of the programs that still form the nucleus of training in all institutes.

My collaboration in this work was very intensive, and the

1. Letter to Franz Alexander, May 13, 1928 (quoted in Jones, vol. 3, pp. 447–8).

training aspect of psychoanalysis became a significant part of my personal experiences. It might be interesting for younger generations of analysts to retrace with me the course of its development. Of course it can be found in the official reports of analytic periodicals; also, Volume III of Ernest Jones' biography of Freud contains a classic description of the history of psychoanalytic training. Still, I think some freshness of view can be gained from the story as told by one who was an active participant.

The forerunner of the Vienna Training Institute was the International Committee on Psychoanalytic Training, whose members were elected by the local organizations belonging to the International Psychoanalytical Association. For several years I was chairman of the training committee of the Vienna Psycho-Analytic Society, so that when the Vienna Training Institute was established in January 1925, largely as an outgrowth of this committee, I was nominated as its director. Siegfried Bernfeld was named vice director, and Anna Freud served as secretary. The further organization of our institute had been discussed at international conferences; this had taken a rather long time, for the proposals were left to be worked out by individual members appointed to this task, who then reported on their preliminary work at the following international congress.

Only when I read Jones' biography of Freud did I learn that Freud had originally opposed the founding of the Vienna Training Institute. He had never expressed these doubts to me, and in our discussions of the problems involved he showed nothing but enthusiasm and readiness to support me in my plans. I have the proud feeling that this was an expression of his confidence in me, and that he changed his original negative opinion after seeing my enthusiasm. My entire energy for this project would certainly have disappeared if I had had the slightest impression that Freud was against it.

Naturally the Training Institute, its organization and its work, was from the very beginning dependent upon decisions made by the International Psycho-Analytical Association, and remained loyal to them. As director, I accepted the authority of the association's general secretary, Dr. Max Eitingon, without ambivalence. Until his death he remained the highest authority, after Freud, on analytic training.

Though it was decided at the time of its foundation that the Vienna Training Institute would be formally independent of the Ambulatorium, the two organizations remained closely connected, as I have already indicated on p. 155.

The Institute was organized under favorable auspices. I had some years of experience in leadership, and Bernfeld was an experienced youth organizer; Anna Freud was loved and admired by all around her. From the beginning Freud was fascinated by Bernfeld's personality—this man seemed to be the very incarnation of the Don Quixote type, even in his external appearance. He was tall and gaunt, with an ugliness that impressed one as beauty. His fanatical adherence to his Zionist ideals led him at times into opportunistic actions, but also made him a spellbinding speaker who converted many enthusiastic young followers to his ideology. In the field of analysis he very soon became a collaborator of Anna Freud, and achieved what no other member of the analytic group had done: he became a training analyst without having had regular analytic training himself.

One of Bernfeld's most devoted pupils was Willi Hofer, who became a beloved friend of every single member of my family —mine as a colleague, Felix's as a pupil, and Martin's as an unofficial teacher. Unfortunately for us, his dedication to his work in England kept him from joining us in America, and we were not with him at the time of his unexpected death. He has stayed in our memories as the young Willi whom we loved so much.

The first years of the Training Institute were not easy ones for me. I had been largely responsible for its creation and had a large emotional investment in its success. I wanted to make it into an international training center second only to the Berlin Training Institute, on which it had been modeled. At Freud's suggestion I had spent the year 1924 in Berlin accumulating information and experience for our institute, and at the same time, on Freud's recommendation, undergoing analysis with Karl Abraham.

I later regretted that my son, then seven years old, paid the heaviest price for my professional progress during this year. My only qualm about going to Berlin was that it would mean a temporary separation of our family. As a compromise, we decided that Martin would spend half of the year with me in Berlin, and half with Felix in Vienna. While he was in Berlin, separated from his father and in a sense neglected by his mother, he had to put up with the strict educational methods of a German governess. Meanwhile his mother was furthering her desire to be the director of a top-ranking training institute.

Freud was completely in accord with the rules of the Vienna Training Institute and did not undertake any didactic analysis without first communicating with the director. He had approved my appointment, and agreed with me on most issues connected with the Institute, which in fact was continuing the methods he himself had used when he was chairman of the Vienna Psycho-Analytic Society.

American analysts usually made contact with the Training Institute through Freud. It is easy to understand that they aspired not only to take the equivalent of postgraduate courses with the famous Viennese specialists, an ambition they shared with the American physicians who came to Vienna, but also to become pupils of Freud. Only in special cases was Freud available; he generally advised these American candidates to contact me. Many of the candidates also came with recommendations to various younger, though well-trained, analysts, and of course we put them in contact with these members of the Institute. One of the candidates began his meeting with me by offering me a letter to Freud that promised quite a substantial amount of money for the Institute. Freud returned this letter to me with a warning: "Be cautious, I do not know what he has in mind—he has a bad reputation." This belief in the power of money was shown by only a small minority of the candidates; and quite a number of outstanding members of American psychoanalytical institutes were trained in Vienna.

Anna Freud made contributions to the Institute as its secretary with her thoroughness, sense of order, and clear and critical thinking. It was she who together with Dr. Edward Bibring took over the directorship of the Institute after I left for America in 1934.

My activities as director were primarily involved with the selection and training of new candidates. I must say that many of my professional enemies who are still living are from the group of candidates who believe I was responsible for their rejection. I was only partly responsible, being only one member of the selection committee. But it is true that my standards for future analysts were very high. In this respect, without even being aware of it, I was in total agreement with Freud.

Official recognition of the Vienna Institute took place at the Ninth International Psychoanalytical Congress in Bad Homburg in 1925, at which I presented a report about the Institute's activity. At this Congress the International Training Commission was founded, with Max Eitingon as chairman. I was elected to this commission, and for the next few years I was very active in it. I had brought up for discussion the problem of control analysis, and I was appointed to work out a general plan.

At the Tenth International Psychoanalytic Congress in Innsbruck in 1927, analytic training and its future course were defined and expressed in three lectures: Sandor Rado's "The Structure of Psychoanalytic Training;" Hanns Sachs' "Training Analysis;" and my "Control Analysis." It was officially announced at the meeting that these three lectures were the foundation of a unified training program for the various institutes and would be published in full in a future issue of the *Zeitschrift.* This promise was not fulfilled, but the ideas expressed in the lectures found realization. Control analysis has become an obligatory part of every psychoanalyst's training. I believe that the program I worked out was my greatest single contribution to the Vienna Training Institute. Meanwhile, Therese Benedek in Chicago had been working on the same problem. She wrote a program for control analysis that was substantially consistent with mine.

Freud, with his strong personal interest in the subject, had laid the foundation for future training programs long before the psychoanalytic movement reached its peak of intensity. As early as 1912, in the second volume of the *Zentralblatt für Psychoanalyse,* he had proposed a technique for the psychoanalytic interpretation of dreams. In 1913, in the first volume of the *Internationale Zeitschrift für Psychoanalyse* he published a series of articles that systematically set forth a complete program of analytic training, together with a discussion of its theoretical basis, which anticipated the later developments in training to an astonishing degree. It is undeniable that everything we, Freud's pupils, have achieved over the years as teachers in the field of training has been accomplished by the application of Freud's ideas.

This is not to say that these ideas have become a petrified heritage. Over the years the methodology of training has developed in the manner of a living organism. Instead of a general director, we now have a dean and specialized committees; the conditions for acceptance of a candidate have been more strictly defined; the problems arising during the training process are solved by persons elected for this purpose; and the selection (from "the pool") of cases to be used in the course of training programs has been relegated to a special committee. As I look back over past developments, I think of how many future generations are going to benefit from Freud's proposals for analytic training! And how many of them are going to say, as I have: "He predicted these developments long ago!"

Looking back further, I am glad that at the beginning of my psychoanalytic career I was ignorant of the controversies and political skirmishes raging around Freud. I learned about them only when I started to attend international meetings regularly and found that there were international politics and conflicts involved. Besides Freud, the one figure of undisputed importance was Max Eitingon, whose idea on training seldom met with opposition. Interestingly enough, I learned at these meetings that one of the main reasons for the professional in-fighting was rivalry for Freud's approval and love.

Now these conflicts have acquired for me a historical and personal importance, as a part of Freud's life. At the time, I was so totally absorbed in my analytic work and so sure of my good relationship with Freud that I kept my naïveté with regard to the politics going on within the international psychoanalytic movement. Freud, who was deprived of recognition in the early years of his work, was burdened with too much of it in later years. He had two battlefields that wasted much of his energy: on the one hand, his adversaries; on the other, his quarreling adherents.

Until my departure from Vienna, my time was divided between the Training Institute and my own clinical work. I was always a clinical psychoanalyst at heart, and my publications in this field have seemed to help others in their work. New clinical experiences continually occupied me; I was especially interested in the so-called hopeless cases—a strong predilection that found its first expression when I was at the Wagner-Jauregg Clinic.

A few unpublished reports still lie in my desk drawer: there was for instance the case of M. (by no means one of the "hopeless" cases), which was especially instructive. Since my search for her over the years has remained fruitless I am fairly certain that she is no longer living. She was a well-known choreographer whose creations represented to me a remarkable combination of infantilism with a highly developed capacity for sublimation. She performed as chief dancer in her own ballet compositions. These dances were always constructed around her; she was the central focus of attention. The other dancers whirled around her; M. confided to me that in her choreography she felt as if she were molding their movements out of some soft malleable material like clay.

Analysis revealed that in her art she was actually exhibiting the child's secret and condemned desire to play with her own feces, now in a form that society not only allowed but even admired. Thus, instead of being a slave to her needs she was absolute ruler of them. She was able to humanize her anal "children" into pupil-dancers obedient to her will, unified with her but at the same time separate. M.'s choreographic work was an expression of her wish to bring forth children from her own body; but it was a highly sublimated expression, subjecting this instinctual drive to the conscious control of artistic performance. Her work as a ballet director was a mature activity, but the ingredients of this activity remained wholly infantile.

Evidently this leap from primitive, instinctual gratification into sublimation was caused by some element that interfered with normal libido development and object relations. No tender, sublimated relationship with her girl pupils had been built up; instead, her relationship with them never surmounted the infantile-narcissistic and instinctual level. It transpired that M.'s persistent infantile relation to her mother on a pre-genital (anal) level was a crucial factor in her artistic endeavors. Furthermore, her mother had had a double function with regard to M.'s future career: training her in bowel control, and later teaching her the discipline of dancing. These two activities combined into a single act in M.'s performances. Such incongruities of development can be found in various guises in various kinds of personalities—in some who are more or less normal as well as in those who are definitely pathological.

Besides the official developments in the psychoanalytic movement, there was something one might call a *Sturm und Drang* revolt of the younger colleagues. It was a movement within a movement arising out of a technical seminar held once a week at our house. It consisted of six married couples: Bibring, Kris,

Hofer, Hartmann, Wälder, and Deutsch. To hide our rebellious purposes, we met on the pretext of playing cards. The game was called the Black Cat and eventually the name was transferred to the group of players. With cards in our hands we sat discussing the latest and most profound problems of psychoanalysis. The "rebellion" was not an ideological departure from Freud; rather, it was the natural impulse of the young to create their own psychological atmosphere in contrast to the conservative older generation. Our group was not directed against contemporary psychoanalysis as such, nor against specific leaders; in fact, it was not "against" anybody.

Even after the events of world politics had dispersed our group, I received touching letters from some of my beloved fellow members of the Black Cat. Unfortunately the group has suffered a sad fate: the male members, who had been pioneers during the most creative period of psychoanalysis, died one after the other, leaving the women alone: Marianne Kris, Grete Bibring, Dora Hartmann, Jenny Wälder-Hall, and me. In the annals of psychoanalysis, all of the female members of the Black Cat have become important figures as writers, teachers, and heads of departments, especially in the field of child psychology. Grete Bibring became full professor of psychiatry at Harvard, and her clinical work at Beth Israel Hospital in Boston has been invaluable in the education of the younger generations of psychiatrists. Marianne Kris, Jenny Wälder-Hall, and Dora Hartmann are among the recognized leaders in child psychiatry. (The Hartmanns had been the last newcomers, and very welcome ones, added to our circle. Heinz Hartmann's background differed from that of the rest: when he joined us he was already a highly esteemed scientist, and though he could have had an outstanding career in official psychiatry, he gave up this chance to become a follower of Freud. He received his compensation through Freud's and Anna Freud's friendship and great respect for him. He made great contributions to ego psychology, using a different approach from that of Anna Freud. In her work Anna Freud emphasized the defense of the ego, whereas Heinz Hartmann concentrated mostly on the so-called "conflict-free sphere." His theories are developed in his chief work, *Essays in Ego Psychology,* as well as in many other publications.)

Freud seems to have known about our group, for when he spoke with me about Felix's and my plans to emigrate to America he mentioned the danger that this productive group would soon fall apart. But in truth it did not fall apart; its members went on working in a new group, with Anna Freud as one of its most active members.

Freud's serious physical illness began in 1923. He had always been very fond of cigars, and suddenly developed an abscess of the gums. Felix, who was then Freud's physician, immediately recognized the abscess as a cancer (leucoplakia). The events that follow are narrated also in Ernest Jones' biography. His account is based on information provided by my husband. Alarmed by his discovery, Felix did not tell Freud the full truth, but did advise Freud to have it removed, and this was done some days later. I remember Felix coming home from this visit very depressed; he stayed in his study until four o'clock in the morning, when he decided to speak with me. Felix's professional discretion urged him not to tell me, but he knew I shared his deep concern and intuitively felt the seriousness of Freud's condition.

Felix told me that Freud had insisted on knowing the truth, but Felix had not dared to tell him immediately, knowing that Freud had a functional heart condition that could be aggravated by a sudden shock. On such occasions, Freud had a tendency to faint. (It is known that Freud fainted once during an encounter with Jung which caused a state of emotional agitation.) When Freud eventually learned the full truth, he reproached my husband for hiding it from him. It was an affront to Freud's ego-ideal to be treated as if he could not face the truth. A tension developed between Felix and Freud; Felix resigned from his position as Freud's personal physician with the explanation that a doctor's most important possession is the full confidence of his patients and that he had obviously lost Freud's. I think my husband never told Freud that he had concealed his diagnosis from fear of precipitating a heart attack, something Freud could not have prevented by willpower. Freud was angry because he believed my husband had underestimated his strength.

The operation was successful, but Freud's mouth had to remain under constant care, and repeated small operations were necessary. My husband continued to have a good relationship with Freud in spite of the disturbing incident; in later years he was even promoted to the status of an old friend. After Professor Königstein's death he became the fourth partner in the weekly card game held at Freud's house. Felix also assisted as a physician during some of the numerous subsequent operations on Freud's mouth. Although Freud had averred many years before that he had "nothing left to say," and now was made a semi-invalid by his illness, he continued to produce significant publications.

Freud always emphasized that his knowledge of people and their neurotic problems stemmed from experiment and direct observation. This is true of his two most revolutionary discoveries: the role of the unconscious and of infantile sexuality in relation to neurosis. Freud's most fundamental papers were of a clinical character: for instance, the earliest of his brilliant clinical works is "Analysis of a Phobia in a Five-Year-Old Boy," for which the child's gifted father, a music critic, had provided the material.[1] But Freud's genius was still needed to draw correct *fundamental* conclusions from these observations.[2]

1. Years later, Freud met "little Hans" again; Hans had grown up to be a fine young man—without neurosis, but with absolutely no memory of his treatment.
2. On the other hand, often an intuitive layman can also draw correct inferences from good observations. When we were traveling in Sicily, I met in our hotel in Taormina a simple schoolteacher who often came from his Saracen village to visit the hotel. He spoke about his pupils and said that if he were to tell me what his observations of them had taught him, I would not believe him. When I insisted on hearing, he told me that he had noted that small boys love their mothers in the same way that grown men love women. He did not know anything about the theory of infantile sexuality; I thereupon gave him a lecture on the Oedipus complex and Freud. The genius and the simple teacher both had the ability to make direct observation a source of significant insights.

In his later years Freud leaned toward the philosophical, speculative aspects of psychoanalysis [1] and thereby encouraged others toward speculation. In retrospect he was moved to remark, "For a short while I allowed myself to leave the sheltered bay of direct experience for speculation. I regret it greatly, for the consequences of so doing do not seem of the best."

The last years of Freud's life and work in Vienna were spent in the shadow of the Nazi regime. During the prewar period Ernest Jones was forming a plan to transfer the Vienna Psycho-Analytical Association *en masse* to England. According to this scheme, Richard Sterba, who was not Jewish and therefore not in any danger from the Nazis, was to stay on in Vienna to represent the Association. Jones' plan was frustrated, however, when most of the members chose for personal reasons to emigrate to America instead of England. My family and I, for example, left for the United States in 1934.

At the time of the Nazi invasion of Vienna, Freud, with typical obstinacy, ignored warnings that he would be in personal danger and remained, like Archimedes, absorbed in his creative work. He did not give up his normal schedule until the Nazis forcibly entered his house and took away whatever money they could find. Freud's famous name and authority would probably have done him no good had not Princess Marie Bonaparte and the American ambassador, W. C. Bullitt, used their influence to help him leave the country.

Before Freud left Vienna for London in 1938, the Nazis demanded from him a written declaration that no harm had been done to him. Even in this situation he did not lose his sense of humor. He wrote out the requested statement, and rumor says that he added an extra sentence, an expression commonly used in Vienna as a character reference for servants: "I would recommend the Gestapo most highly to anyone." I know, however, that Freud expressed this joke verbally, not in writing.

1. *Civilization and Its Discontents,* trans. James Strachey (New York: W.W. Norton & Company, 1962).

On his arrival in London, Freud bought a very suitable house, in which he lived until his death. It is presently the lifelong residence of Anna Freud and a museum for Freud's archaeological collection. The city of London has put up a blue plaque to commemorate Freud's residence there.

In London Anna founded the now world-famous Hampstead Clinic, which became an international center for training in child analysis. She had already worked with psychically disturbed children in Vienna, along with August Eichhorn and Siegfried Bernfeld. I remember that once she tried to persuade me to work with children, but I was then of the opinion that the path to problem children led through an understanding of the normal child. I had such knowledge only as a mother, and besides I had not seemed an especially apt learner while acquiring it.

Freud's sixteen years of suffering after the first operation on his mouth were ended by his death on September 23, 1939, not long after his arrival in London. From Anna's letters and other personal reports we learned that he had undergone repeated operations, but had always returned undaunted to his work and to the things that gave him pleasure. In one of Anna's letters, she reported that Freud had just come back from a walk, the first one after his twenty-ninth operation; he was delighted with the fresh air after the rain. He accepted his sufferings patiently, and nothing could destroy his capacity to enjoy even the most modest gifts of life.

XII

America

MY RELATIONSHIP with America began in 1930, when the American philanthropist Clifford W. Beers invited nine prominent European psychiatrists to attend, as his guests, the first International Congress on Mental Hygiene in Washington, D.C. The visiting psychiatrists were to present a series of seminars and lectures according to a previously established program developed for social workers, doctors, and educators. My preparations required several weeks of my time, for I was not yet fluent in English.

This was my first voyage across the Atlantic. The ship, the *Bremen,* was luxuriously decorated. Among my fellow passengers were several famous German professors of psychiatry and three other psychoanalysts. We had the honor of sitting at the captain's table; my childhood dreams of glory seemed to be coming true.

I had a taste of American journalism as soon as the ship docked at the pier. Reporters swarmed aboard and I was interviewed like a prima donna. The next day my picture appeared on the front page of the New York *Herald Tribune* with the caption:

A Lady-in-Waiting at the Freudian Court, Dr. Helene Deutsch has just visited America—the first accredited ambassador of her sex to come here from the King of Psycho-Analysis.

I did not succeed during the rest of my stay in warding off this sort of journalism, nor did I have any way of communicating to the public that these reports concerning Freud and my relationship to him had not originated with me. "Lady-in-waiting" was the last thing I wanted to be called, though I had always been very proud of being one of Freud's pupils.

The lordly welcome continued in New York. I was ushered into a suite in the Hotel Roosevelt, which in those days was still one of the most elegant hotels in the city; here journalists and a crowd of women, mostly leaders in the field of social work, had gathered to meet me. A schedule of lectures to be given by me was thrust into my hands—and at that moment I realized that this was not, after all, the trip of a star.

Of course I had already met a few American social workers who had come to Vienna to learn about psychoanalysis. But I hadn't known how important a role these earnest and industrious women played in furthering social welfare in their own country. Later on, after we came to America ourselves, my husband devoted much of his time and energy to the education of social workers. For several years he gave up his vacation to give summer courses for them. His lectures were subsequently published in many journals in the field of social work, and they still enjoy great popularity.

When one travels to a foreign land one usually plans what to take along, spiritually and realistically. I brought with me Freud's true teachings, considerable clinical experience, and a proud awareness that I was a personal pupil of Freud. Besides this, I brought with me, as one always does on major voyages, both old and new fantasies. I consider "old" the ones that were bound up with my childhood. In my native country, America was considered the land of quickly won fortunes, the realm of the millionaires. The vision of inexhaustible gold lured even

Christopher Columbus when he discovered America. And so although America became a geographic, historical reality, at the same time it remained a symbol of wealth and of boundless possibility and a dream for all the deprived and rejected of Europe.

I remember Uncle L., who went to America and soon sent back to my mother a symbol of his newly acquired riches: an umbrella with a golden handle. For many immigrants, America was a disappointment. Often the poor Polish peasants who were enticed there by exaggerated reports found nothing but further exploitation, although some of them did attain prosperity.

I knew about the battles between the Indians and the white settlers from my childhood reading. Naturally these books depicted the Indians as the villains and the whites as the heroes; but I was always on the Indians' side, and I regarded America in general as an exploiter.

Nonetheless, America was also the country where one could find refuge when fleeing from the military draft or from imprisonment. One also remembered the Revolutionary War and the Polish revolutionary hero Kosciuszko. From that time on, America was a haven for refugees persecuted in their own countries. In more recent times it sheltered Jews fleeing from Nazi persecution in Europe.

My second and final trip to America was in September 1934, when I left Vienna with my son to settle in the United States. (My husband had to stay in Vienna until the end of the year in order to fulfill his professional duties, but Martin had to be in America before the next college semester began.) Nobody knew how terribly I grieved at having to leave not only Freud but also everything I held dear in psychoanalysis. Why did I do it? I was seeking security—but not primarily for myself and my husband. For a long time I had been in a state of extreme anxiety about our beloved son.

Martin, filled with revolutionary zeal, had been very active in the Viennese students' political resistance to the reactionary Dollfuss regime. It was Freud himself who alerted us to the dangers of these activities. My husband had also been warned by an old school friend who had become a professor in Martin's high school. We thought Martin would be safe if we sent him off to a boarding school, the famous Schuloch School in Zürich. Here he gained his *Abitur* in 1933 at the age of seventeen and matriculated at the Technical Institute of Zürich. Meanwhile he remained in close contact with his friends in Vienna.

Once again it was Freud, whose kind concern extended not only to his pupils but also to their families, who alerted us to the danger that still threatened Martin. Switzerland was not far enough away from Vienna to afford adequate protection.

Our thoughts of moving to America became even more serious after my husband, on a lecture tour in America in 1933, saw better than we could in Vienna the danger that Nazism posed for Austria. Furthermore, Dr. Robert Wälder's unusually acute historical sense made him advise us, even then, not to buy a farm we had been interested in; later events proved him right. At the time, his advice caused me great disappointment, for I had expected this farm to be the fulfillment of a vision we had always shared.

In such an atmosphere of insecurity and worry, it was not surprising that my husband accepted the invitation of Dr. Stanley Cobb to help him establish a center for psychosomatic research in his psychiatric department in Massachusetts General Hospital in Boston. Dr. Cobb made it clear that his research grant covered only one year's work. We decided to make a one-year visit to America, without any further plans. Later political developments in Europe were to cause us to prolong this visit.

Before I left for America, I went for a last visit to my real home—to say farewell to Przemyśl, to the Gizowski house, to the hills of *Schlossberg*. I wanted to see these scenes of my childhood and youth, but I wanted also to show the ghosts of those whom I had never ceased to love dearly that the wayward Hala had grown up and achieved, but was still faithful to the enchantments of her past: her father's love, the melody of the "Marseillaise," and that bearer of the banner of freedom whom I have designated "L." Throughout my life, Przemyśl was to remain for me the symbol of my genuine identity, as well as of my impetus to grow.

After a year of study at the Technical Institute in Zürich it had become clear to Martin that this was not the best place for him. He was sure that America could offer him better educational prospects in physics. His decision to enter an American college was responsible for our rushed departure in September 1934: we wanted to arrive before the beginning of the college semester. In this hospitable land Martin had the choice of beginning his studies at Harvard or at M.I.T. He decided on M.I.T., where he eventually became a full professor of physics.

Martin had made his plans independently from us, ruled by his own interest in physics. In fact, he regarded my company on the voyage to the United States as an unnecessary burden. I had forgotten that despite his intellectual maturity he was still deeply enmeshed in the problems of late adolescence. An ocean voyage into the blue yonder with one's mother is not too alluring! He combatted the psychologically unfavorable situation by completely avoiding my company and immediately attaching himself to a girl his age.

The ship offered me a small comfort: down below in the third-class cabins, a distinguished American woman was sitting like a queen in the company of the working-class European immigrants. I went in search of her, bearing a letter of introduction from her daughter, Dr. Julia Deming, who was a colleague of mine; I found her among the poorest Italian workers, chatting and playing cards. She turned out to be a very interesting eccentric, and a good companion throughout the voyage.

We already had friends in Boston to whom we could turn with full confidence. I'm not speaking only of Dr. Fritz Wittels, who had emigrated to the United States long before the political unrest had begun and had been largely responsible for my sensational reception in New York on my first visit. There were many Americans who had at some point gone to Vienna for analysis, some as patients, others as students. I can even say that on my arrival I had already filled up in advance almost all of my professional office hours with patients seeking analysis.

My favorite hostesses were my former pupils Helen Ross and Marian Putnam. Helen had a special position among my analysands: I had diagnosed her as a unique case of freedom from neurosis. She later became a professor of child psychology at the University of Chicago, which recently established the Helen Ross Professorship in Child Psychology in her honor. Her empathy with children and a strong need for activity made her a very productive worker in her field. Her work when I first met her centered on adolescent girls, for whom she had established her famous girls' camp on Footprint Island in Michigan. Her contact with psychoanalysis made her realize that to be successful in her work with children she needed more clinical experience. She became a pupil of Anna Freud and since then has spent a part of every year working at the Hampstead Clinic in London in close collaboration with Anna. In addition, she has written with Bertram Lewin a thorough study of the psychoanalytic training institutes in the United States, based on direct personal investigation.[1] The impact of her personality has been widely felt in the American psychoanalytic movement. She has exerted a great deal of practical influence also; when a worthy cause stands in need of financial help, one turns automatically to Helen, who can move mountains and foundations into action with her wisdom and kindness.

Marian Putnam was the founder and supporter of the James Putnam Children's Center in Roxbury, Massachusetts. In her humanitarian spirit, Molly originally planned a home for wayward youths. The collaboration of Beata Rank in this project diverted her interest toward "atypical" children—small children with psychotic disturbances. Molly worked hard and very successfully, hiding her great compassion for humanity under her

1. Bertram D. Lewin and Helen Ross, *Psychoanalytic Education in the United States* (New York: W.W. Norton & Company, 1960).

modesty and discretion. The sentence "If it weren't for Molly Putnam. . . ." became a slogan for many.

I must confess that Molly's recent death has changed to some degree the spirit of this writing. But I have to remind myself that though Molly herself suffered losses during the years of our friendship and collaboration, these never changed the quality of the work in which she was engaged. When I say, "Planted trees have to grow," I mean that the fruits of the earth have to blossom in spite of the grieving of their planter . . . this was Molly. If I include myself in this part of Molly's life, it was because of her blessed influence on me. Our friendship was a happy interchange I shall never cease to miss.

From the very first I taught courses for social workers under the auspices of the Psychoanalytic Society, together with my American colleagues. (I must emphasize that it was my husband whose work with social workers and whose publications in this field had a permanent influence.) My courses seemed to be popular, and certain pronouncements of mine, which I don't remember ever having made, are still in circulation. Once, for instance, these conscientious women had a question for me that is still of great significance: which takes precedence in the administration of social welfare—the client's financial condition or the neurosis that is often at the bottom of his social misery? According to the story my answer was, "When in doubt, buy him a pair of shoes."

Even before I arrived in Boston, I had decided it belonged to that part of the world in which one could live free of anti-Semitism. Though I was still full of homesickness and a growing nostalgic desire somehow to go back, I was determined to speed up the assimilation process and began immediately to look for a home. Imagine my astonishment when here too I unexpectedly encountered anti-Semitism as the manager of a stately apartment complex in Brookline expressed his scruples at taking in immigrant Jews. Dr. Irmarita Putnam, a distinguished colleague, was helping me look for a place to live. I had known her since her student years with Freud in Vienna, and on my arrival in Boston she had placed herself and her chauffeur completely at my disposal. After this incident she brought me to the Hotel Commander in Cambridge, where we spent the first year of our stay in Boston—that is, my husband and I; Martin from the beginning lived in his own apartment near M.I.T.

Gradually it became clear to Felix and me that it would be impossible for us to return to Vienna, and eventually I informed Freud of this, my heart full of sorrow and guilty feelings. His answer to my letter was sent out on the day Hitler invaded Vienna; this fact makes it not only a significant keepsake for me but also an important historical document. The letter was stamped with a special official Nazi date stamp bearing in the center a swastika with the phrase around it, *Der Führer in Wien.* Of course my reaction to this stamp was one of fury against Hitler and a sense of guilt because I was not there; this feeling did not disappear completely until I was certain that Freud and his family were safe in London. Freud's letter helped to soothe my guilt, but it increased my love and longing for him. In it Freud expressed astonishment that I should ask for his forgiveness "without saying what for." The last sentence reads, "I rely on your assurance that you have remained true to analysis, and hope with you that you will accomplish no less good there [in America] than you have accomplished here." I interpreted these words as a mission given to me by Freud which I automatically tried to fulfill. Have I succeeded in this mission?

Before Freud's expectations could be realized, I had to establish myself professionally. My work in America could not be a simple continuation of my work in Vienna. It had to be an application of psychoanalysis to a new external world. Psychoanalysis in America already had a history filled with great names: James Putnam, H. W. Frink, Smith Ely Jelliffe, A. A. Brill, and others. All of them were either official and active members of the movement or at least ideologically in sympathy with it.

With the flight to the United States of great numbers of refugees from Europe's scientific community before and during

World War II, American acceptance of European psychoanalysis increased enormously. The application of psychoanalysis to educational and social problems found a much larger field of operation in America. For the European analysts who came to the United States as latter-day pioneers, the chief activity was the teaching of psychoanalysis, which led to the establishment of training institutes generally patterned after the one in Vienna. All of us participated in the organization of training in America —the seminars, discussion groups, controls,—and the establishment of criteria for the acceptance of candidates. We accepted this assignment willingly, all the more so because many of us had had the rich experience of doing our own pioneering work in psychoanalysis in Europe. Of course the European procedures had to be adjusted to American conditions and needs.

In general, most of the newcomers found what they were seeking. Some found careers; others fitted into institutions suited to the development of their talents; all of them found a relatively secure financial situation. Those who loved money found ways to grow rich; and impressive social positions were achieved by those who appreciated prestige. My husband and I also found what we were seeking: the opportunity of unhindered work. For Felix, this was mainly in psychosomatic medicine; for me it had to do with a variety of neurotic problems.

In this connection I must mention Erik Erikson, another outstanding personality from Vienna who was here when Felix and I came to Boston. Erikson had attended one of my seminars at the Vienna Psycho-Analytic Society and I was glad to be remembered in his biography as one of his teachers. I also knew his gifted and beautiful wife as a student of dance in Vienna even before she met Erik. After a number of very productive years in Boston Erikson went to San Francisco, where he became a professor of psychology at Berkeley without himself having had a university education. Like Thomas Mann, he was self-educated (Mann had worked for his *Abitur* only in order to shorten his term of required military service.) Erikson was one of the Berkeley faculty members who refused to sign the oath of allegiance required by the university. The Eriksons eventually returned to Boston, and Erik has helped me more than once in situations with young people that I was not able to handle alone. Over and above the fame he has achieved in America, Erikson has shown himself by his deeds to be not only an artist and a powerful intellect but a person with compassion for individual destinies. I am glad to have an opportunity here to express my awareness of these qualities and my respect for him.

In Boston, an established psychoanalytic society already existed, but the organized teaching of analysis was only in its beginning stages. Dr. Hanns Sachs had come to Boston in 1932 as the chosen envoy of Freud at the invitation of Irmarita Putnam, a former analysand of Freud. Sachs became in effect the official training analyst of the Boston Psychoanalytic Society. In my opinion (which is shared by others), Sachs did not quite succeed in this mission. He did not find it necessary to communicate with the young members of the Society; and, against all the rules of the international training organizations, he chose his own training candidates according to his quite personal criteria. His refusal to consult with the locally elected leaders of the Society had a very negative effect on the young organization. Sachs' deficient understanding of neurosis may not have interfered with his understanding of analytical theory, but it certainly impaired his practical use of theory. Many of the representatives of psychoanalysis in Boston felt disappointed and critical, knowing that he lacked essential clinical experience.

Despite his shortcomings, Sachs had excellent intellectual qualities and a high degree of culture, which made him one of Freud's chosen pupils. He was an excellent raconteur, especially of Jewish jokes. He had many friends and admirers, but I personally felt resentment that he refused to show more consideration and respect for the younger generation of analysts.

Sachs' influence was somewhat balanced by that of other European analysts—for instance, Herman Nunberg, who had come to

New York at the invitation of the New York Psychoanalytic Society, and Franz Alexander, invited to Boston by Augusta Healy and William Bronner. Also, Boston proved especially attractive to many good, even outstanding, newcomers, some of them my Viennese friends and pupils. The Black Cat did not come as a unit, but my fantasy looked forward to the possibility of regrouping once more. Unfortunately it took a long series of anxieties and uncertainties before the few survivors of the group could revive their former attachments; psychoanalysts proved to be no different from other refugees throughout history. As for myself, I had to accept the resentment of some of my previous friends: I was secure at a time when they were homeless. As time went on, the older and younger newcomers reached emotional agreement among themselves, as well as with those whose land they had invaded; we became their pupils and they became ours.

I have already mentioned that the historical development of psychoanalysis in America has been traced in a book by Helen Ross and Bertram Lewin (p. 177). My account of psychoanalytic teaching in America will be extremely cursory, since it is not my intention to write such a history in this book. As to my personal contribution, I was a member of a number of committees, where I tried to do my best in a frame of activity very different from my work in Vienna. As a member of the Boston Society-Institute I obeyed its rules, but for many years I did not avoid the controversies that blossomed in its committees.

One of these had to do with the problem of lay analysis, which was renewed in America after being solved (or rather fought through) in Europe. Lay analysts (candidates without a medical degree) were eventually accepted by most of the psychoanalytic societies in America, and definite training programs were set up to prevent the intrusion of inadequately prepared candidates. Of course the candidates with medical training also have to fulfill strict conditions of acceptance.

Another controversy which for a time absorbed the energies of both younger and older analysts was the "Bill of Rights" passed by Congress after World War II, which granted to young psychiatrists who were war veterans the opportunity to receive analytic training. They had privileges identical with those of war veterans in other fields, and the financial support of their psychoanalytic training was taken over by the government. Without going deeper into the technicalities of the disputes that arose, I will only mention the central problem: are the psychoanalytic institutes primarily for *treatment* of the candidate or for his *training?* The real answer is that analysis is both, simultaneously: the candidates had their personal neurotic problems, which sometimes made their analysis more therapeutic than didactic. The question was academic but it was also practical, because the veterans had an advantage over others: their analysis was paid for by the government. This sometimes caused embarrassment to the Institute, as it was difficult to reject a candidate when rejection would deprive him of the compensation stemming from his position as a veteran.

The other major problem was that the young veteran doctors who qualified academically for this training were not necessarily always qualified as personalities. I remind you of my earlier statement that Freud considered a candidate's character as the main condition for his acceptance. The development of analysis has had its periods of struggle, and the one I have just discussed was certainly not the last.

I learned more about the important connection between psychoanalysis and its social applications through the Judge Baker Foundation and its two directors, William Healy and Augusta Bronner. I don't think I met either of them when I made my first visit to America. They were fairly well acquainted with Freud's writings when they came, later on, to Vienna to learn more about psychoanalysis, but they had only three months to spend and realized that much more time was required for a personal didactic analysis. I let them know that I was willing to try to demonstrate the technique of psychoanalysis using their own dreams and associations as teaching material. I was quite satisfied with the results of this experiment. The book they later published, *The Structure and Meaning of Psychoanalysis as Related to Personality and Behavior,*[1] clearly shows that they had gained enough understanding of the whole process of psychoanalysis to know *how it is done,* even without ever having actively practiced it themselves. They remained well-disposed towards analysis, and their attitude was of great value to our younger colleagues who worked at Judge Baker.

Several generations of capable psychiatrists, psychologists, youth workers, etc., have studied and taught at Judge Baker. After Healy's death, my friendship with Augusta Bronner continued until she eventually withdrew from public life. Dr. George Gardner became a worthy heir of these two pioneers, and under his direction Judge Baker continued to fulfill its great social and didactic mission.

Two women colleagues of mine who were analyzed by Dr. Hanns Sachs were Dr. Eleanor Pavenstedt and Dr. Florence Wislocki-Clothier. They remained faithful to analysis and, what was of great value to me, they also remained my personal friends. I am indebted to both of them for much of the material having to do with the problems of adolescence, adoption, unmarried mothers, stepmotherhood, etc., that appears in the two volumes of *The Psychology of Women,* and that I had not been able to study to my own satisfaction during my years in Vienna. It was not that these problems didn't exist there; but they were kept as far as possible out of the public eye.

In those years Dr. Pavenstedt was a very promising beginner in psychoanalysis. Now she is one of the greatest authorities on the psychology of small children growing up under conditions of social deprivation. She has written with Dr. Lucie Jessner a series of psychiatric studies of children. Her fame comes chiefly from a book *The Drifters,* written in collaboration with Dr. Charles Malone. For me, however, Eleanor's most important activity is our Wednesdays, which we try to spend extravagantly,

1. New York: A.A. Knopf, 1946.

usually at a movie followed by dinner at my house or an exotic restaurant.

Dr. Lucie Jessner, a close personal friend, still considers herself one of my pupils. She tells me that she attended my clinical lectures and seminars at the Boston Psychoanalytic Institute, and remembers from those not only the results of my psychiatric experiences but also my empathy with the patients and with the candidates. She herself was continuing at the Institute the training she had started in Switzerland. It did not take me long to discover that Lucie was a person of great culture and unusual psychological empathy; though modest and unobtrusive, in her quiet way she communicates clearly the power of her intelligence. She on her part reports that she has learned very much from me. As for me, I think that the enrichment of our understanding of the psychological problems of neurotic people was entirely reciprocal. Lucie's professional development brought her to child analysis, which became the center of her interests; she has published very important papers in this field. But she has always retained her great capacity to understand the psychic problems of adults as well. I have never met anybody who knows Lucie— juvenile or elderly, "important" or obscure—who was not lovingly devoted to her. I sometimes compare her to a musical instrument with great richness of tone, answering the emotional "music" of the other person sensitively, in that person's own emotional tones. Lucie can make people, the sick and the healthy, secure and happy in the feeling that she understands them and their problems.

Her power of empathy also endows her with a deep cognizance of other fields of art, with a special emphasis on literature. Before she became a student of medicine, she had a doctoral degree in literature. She herself has always had something in her external appearance that makes one think of an artistic creation— a delicate beauty that has resisted the destructiveness of time.

Besides the Psychoanalytic Society-Institute, the second sphere of my professional activity in Boston was Dr. Stanley Cobb's psychiatric clinic at Massachusetts General Hospital, where my husband had been entrusted with the task of organizing a psychosomatic department. For a long period in Vienna, following my retirement from the Wagner-Jauregg Clinic, I had had to do without hospital practice. This new opportunity to participate in clinical conferences and hospital rounds was very exciting, bringing me into contact not only with current developments in American psychiatry but also with people from diverse social backgrounds. What fascinated me most about this hospital was the respect accorded to the patients. Obviously it was here that the dynamic personality of Dr. Cobb was decisive.

In our very first conversation Dr. Cobb wanted to know about my future plans, and asked me whether I had an academic career in mind. My first reaction was to remember an earlier conversation with Wagner-Jauregg in which he told me sympathetically that the Ministry of Education in Vienna wasn't prepared "just yet" to confer an academic title on a woman. When I asked Dr. Cobb what I needed an academic career for, he answered with one word: "Prestige." I candidly admitted to him that this word did not loom large in my vocabulary, since if I took it seriously it would mean a narrowing of my personal liberty. Dr. Cobb understood me, because he too was not a prestige-seeker and was extremely modest about his influential position.

The influx of candidates increased constantly at the Boston Training Institute, and so did my workload. But rather than trying to reduce this burden I began to look for new activities connected with psychoanalysis. From an early age I had always liked to avoid the highways and investigate the side roads. Thus I became involved in a fascinating project that compensated for a great many other activities I had to give up. This was known as the Hunter Green Project. It had evolved from an idea of Dr. Sam Gutman, who owned an estate in Hunter Green, near Princeton. Together with Dr. Muriel Gardner, he organized gifted analysts from different parts of the country into groups that met on his estate and conducted seminars on an advanced level. The participants were chosen to be neither too old nor too young; and they did in fact represent the intellectual elite among the future leaders of psychoanalysis.

I do not know whether the Hunter Green Project—a kind of postgraduate course with selectively admitted participants—is still functioning or whether there are other similar unofficial organizations. Here, in contrast to official teaching, participants could choose special, usually difficult scientific problems of psychoanalysis for discussion. I enjoyed these meetings, in which I functioned not only as a teacher but also as a pupil inspired by the high level of our discussions.

I was also invited by the San Francisco Psychoanalytic Institute to give a series of seminars and lectures there. I felt that this visit was a great success for all concerned; some of the members of this Institute stayed in contact with me for a long time, sending me their papers and communicating their problems. Thus through both these projects I came into contact with the groups active outside of Boston, and with their leading personalities.

These extra activities came at the right moment in my professional life. After more than twenty years of complete devotion to the teaching of candidates in training institutes, I felt tired. In all other scientific and professional fields there exists the opportunity to take a sabbatical after six years of work. This seems impossible for an active psychoanalyst, but I felt in myself the urgent need to do something different. More and more I turned toward nonprofessional activities. I had the feeling that America offered more possibilities than Vienna for escape from my all-absorbing professional life.

XIII

Babayaga

MY HUSBAND and I had bought a small house in Cambridge that we adapted to our needs by making additions. Finally we had something we had never had in Vienna: our own house and a garden. A house in Cambridge naturally came with neighbors and the American neighborly atmosphere. We were greeted warmly with the words, "We don't resent Jews like *you!*" As I heard them, I thought of the saying of a well-known anti-Semitic *Bürgermeister* of Vienna: "I'll decide who's a Jew and who isn't." It was all so paradoxical. I was born in anti-Semitic Poland and grew up in Vienna during its most intense anti-Semitic phase, but it was only in America that I encountered personal anti-Semitism for the first time.

Soon after this we decided to act on the widely accepted view that nothing makes an exile feel more at home than possessing a piece of rural earth in the new country. I had dreamed of this piece of land when we were still young doctors in Vienna and rented a small part of a poor farmhouse in southern Austria, but we possessed no land of our own. Now that we had the chance of becoming wealthy Americans (though it became obvious that we had no talent to effect this change ourselves) this dream came closer to its realization. The old wish had a new emotional element: we felt a painful longing for the countryside we had left on the other side of the Atlantic.

Our first guides around New England were scientist friends from Chicago who had made a hill in Vermont their summer home. We accepted their invitation to visit, and during our stay we thought we were back in the Tyrol again. As soon as we could, we bought a piece of land that was still available, complete with a rickety old house, and reveled in the feeling that now we were in a Tyrol without Nazis! However, we soon realized that we wouldn't be able to use the house for weekend trips: the six-hour drive from Boston was too wearing. After a few months we sold it back to the original owner for the same price we had paid, but we didn't give up our search.

Our friend and colleague Dr. Jack Murray had a piece of property in Wolfeboro, New Hampshire, on the shore of the popular and noisy Lake Winnipesaukee. This is a large lake with many resorts, motorboats, and all the summer holiday apparatus we were trying to avoid. But in our explorations of the neighborhood we found, on a hill about eleven miles out of town, the perfect refuge from this clamor: a somewhat neglected farm that still retained traces such as those that make one say of an older woman: "Once she was very beautiful."

We bought the farm at once, changed its old family name "Chamberlain Farm" to "Babayaga Farm," and had only one regret: it was not on the water and we were enthusiastic swimmers. A solution was soon found: the hill on which our new property lay was located between two lakes, Winnipesaukee and Wentworth. On Lake Wentworth we usually saw only brightly colored sailboats. (Later on, unfortunately, the inevitable motorboats arrived.) Lake Wentworth shared with the farm the most splendid sunsets. We bought a large piece of land along its shore, and after removing the boulders from the bank of the lake, we made a sandy beach with imported sea sand. We also built a large bathhouse, big enough to live in. Now we had a double haven: one on the tip of a small hill and one by the lake. The sunsets on the farm can only be compared with those I saw in my childhood in Przemyśl over the hills of the *Schlossberg*.

By this time Martin had married, thus fulfilling my husband's desire for a daughter. Felix accepted Suzanne fully in this role. Suzanne was at the time studying to become a psychiatric social worker. Later, feeling that there were already enough psychiatrists in the family, she changed to medical social work, concentrating on the problems of old age. Armed with a knowledge of both fields, she stayed active in her profession, interrupted only by the periods in which she was needed more as a mother for her two sons than as a social worker.

Of course we had to provide Martin and his family with a home on the farm. Beside the old farmhouse—whose bright new appearance made one think of the umbrella that has from time to time received a new covering, and then again a new handle, but is still called "the old umbrella"—arose a second, genuinely new house for the younger generations. Of course the third generation took over both houses completely, with the smiling consent of their grandparents. Our family still owns Babayaga Farm, and we continue to regard it as one of the paradises of this life, which is shadowed only by the loss of our beloved Felix.

In those early days a real farmer was very much needed at Babayaga. Felix was appointed to fill that need for the time being, despite his other preoccupations. For instance, he had made the old henhouse into a studio in which he painted many beautiful pictures for the children and, without my knowledge, worked on his scientific writings.

We bought the farm for purposes of rest and relaxation, but my hidden intention—call it fantasy—was to use it as a permanent refuge from psychoanalysis. It was to be a kind of sabbatical without limitations, although I had no doubt that my identification with psychoanalysis was so ingrained that no incognito could really be strong enough to overcome it.

Babayaga did not remain purely a vacation retreat for long. We, the recent European immigrants, did some pioneering work between the small cemetery in the center of the fields, where the bones of old Yankee families lay beneath fallen gravestones, and the wide stone wall encircling the property, where luxuriant grasses grew in the days before the wall fell completely into ruins. We changed the rocky fields into real meadows and enlivened them with handsome cows, sheep, and goats.

In the course of our travels in New England we had seen many modernized farms. We decided to renovate our beautiful ancient barn somewhat, but preserve its character. The clean and hygienic stalls for six cows were provided with a modern, automatic water supply; there was a special compartment for the cows' calving, and an electric milking machine. Later on we also had a perfect farmer, Jeff, whom we hired to look after the farm in our absence. The old farm office became a separate house for our older grandson Peter; Nicholas, the younger one, took over the pigpen as his palace. Meanwhile the pigs received a new house built specially for them over the newly dug vegetable cellar.

During World War II we, the European intellectuals, went back to Mother Earth, and were more welcome to this war-weary and hungry world as farmers than as scholars.[1] Dr. Molly Putnam, who from childhood on had been very interested in farming, took over the responsibility for our agricultural blunders (hers and mine) during the year that Felix was filling a one-year appointment as director of an institute for psychosomatic research he had organized in St. Louis. On the farm, I specialized in observation of the animals, and Dr. Putnam dealt with the business aspects. For instance, she took our eggs to Cambridge and went from one beautiful old Cambridge house to another, selling eggs at the market price to her Harvard-Radcliffe friends.

1. During the war Martin was working, along with many other research physicists, at the Los Alamos testing ground, which was to become famous as the birthplace of the atomic bomb. During this time the gates of Los Alamos were closed to visitors, and we could see him and his wife Suzanne only at rare intervals. The gates themselves reminded me of the time just after World War I when my father came to see his grandson at the gate erected between the Austrian and Polish sectors of Vienna.

We felt that we were important members of the community, ignoring the fact that our expenses were substantial: by our own estimate they amounted to about one dollar per egg!

Our buying of livestock was highly unprofessional. We chose the cows according to our aesthetic feelings (we preferred cows with beautiful eyes). Since our cows were wonderfully fed, as a courtesy to us they produced milk of especially high quality. Jeff was not too thorough in making butter and cream, so that the milk contained a high proportion of butterfat and everyone said it tasted like cream. Thus we at least had a market for the milk, although the cows remained a luxury.

Molly planted strawberries, and this enterprise was a double success: not only were the berries delicious, but she also acquired the name "Strawberry Molly" with our grandchildren—a name she has kept throughout twenty years. For years Molly remained in contact with the farm and with strawberries. The apples in the ancient orchard and the narcissus growing along the little pond still speak to us about the beautiful years when we still had our Molly. Her recent death has left me with the feeling that Babayaga Farm can never again be what it once was. Our grandsons, who, when they were little boys, would help her if not in planting then in eating the strawberries, grieve with me . . . Strawberry Molly.

Despite my work on the farm I didn't give up my intellectual identity entirely: in the middle of the meadows I built a *Nansenhäuschen*—a place where I could observe the farm's animal mothers and their young (the children later named it "Granny's Folly"). All of this was quite expensive, but then I also learned a great deal, generally things our wise old farmer Jeff had already known for a long time; for example, that when pigs eat their young during a thunderstorm, they aren't doing this because they are "swine" but rather from the instinct to shelter their brood within the mother's body. Or that when a cow licks her newborn calf to clean off the birth fluids, she does it because her own body needs these substances; and so on. All the information provided by Jeff was confirmed by professional agriculturalists who had great respect for Jeff's practical experience. My own observations served as a good corrective to my former misconceptions and provided me with a wealth of new knowledge, banal though it might seem to professionals in animal husbandry.

I saw in myself a conflict of interest between my intellectual preoccupations and my emotional self. I felt like the personification of a children's song my grandsons loved: A peculiar creature turns up in a chicken yard. She feels out of place and unwanted, and moves on to the goose yard. But here too she is greeted by protesting cackles. In despair she asks herself, "Who am I? I am not a chicken, I am not a goose. I am a chirkendoose!" My grandsons enjoyed this song without knowing how much their grandmother identified herself with this strange animal.

At this point I must introduce Jenny, our pet hen, who always stayed with people rather than in the henhouse, and who one day fell victim to a new neighbor, a fox who every night made off with one of our hens. The morning that Jenny too disappeared, we all felt bereaved, as though we had lost a favorite dog or cat. But Jenny loved life with us too much to let a mere fox kill her off. She returned, covered with blood, and we heard no more of the fox! Evidently Jenny was not one of those creatures that are easily preyed upon by others.

I could tell more stories of my animal studies, but I'd be ashamed of what Jeff, our farmer, would think; he regarded me as dreadfully naïve. And I could fill more than just this book with stories of the farm, if it weren't sure to bore my readers; especially stories of our catastrophes. For instance, there was our water problem. It was very "civilized" to have two bathrooms in each of our two houses; but our water shortage soon became evident when one of our guests complained that there hadn't been enough water for his morning bath. This meant that we had to have an artesian well dug. The tension associated with this project can be known only by those who have shared the experience: you dig farther and farther down, and with each yard the price of the job goes higher. We stood, the whole family, around the chasm. Finally—after two hundred yards! It's not true that one can withdraw to the country and take a vacation from the cares of civilization. We drag our civilized needs along with us wherever we go.

I should add that for a long time we piped in the animals' water supply from our artesian well, and discovered only later that there was a big pond, overgrown with weeds, in the middle of the fields!

Only our egg industry survived the decline of our farming. We eventually sold the cows but kept the chicken houses, and for quite a number of years we had an average of four hundred chickens. Only the death of my husband brought the nearly total abandonment of the farming "business." Now only the apple harvest and my son's woodchopping remind us that the beautiful and well-kept houses on the grounds of Babayaga once belonged not to academicians but to real Yankees.

I think the time has come to reveal the incognito of Babayaga, after whom the farm was named. What is the relationship of Babayaga to me, the would-be farmwife immersed in her scientific and professional work? Her Polish name seems to give away the secret: Babayaga is *me,* and the legend of this Polish witch leads directly back to my childhood. In Polish folklore, Babayaga is a good witch who is especially kind to children; she is also a rustic witch, usually seen carrying on her back a load of wood, and sometimes children. Thus both my love for my grandchildren and my fantasies about being a country woman have fitted in very well with this figure; she is the prototype of the kind grandmother, even though her mode of transportation is a broom and her passageway the chimney. I told the children many stories about my role as a witch, and I think that Babayaga is to them, even today, associated with their real Granny and beloved "Gruhu."

Babayaga, being timeless, is still haunting our farm in Wolfeboro; there she can be seen flying on her broom and disappearing into the clouds. When the sky clears, only a small silvery-white cloudlet remains high up in the sky, and then dissolves into the air—just as the aging farmers of New England are disappearing and being replaced by a younger generation of gentleman farmers and their complicated machinery.

I must include in this autobiography a few pages about my real travels, by airplane instead of by broomstick, for they have been an important part of my life. Most of my journeys, especially those of my younger days, were in part the expression of a sublimated drive toward knowledge and experience—the projection, as for many other people, of an inner tension that finds a release in curiosity about the outside world. In the fairly common phenomenon of runaway children, flight from the home is often the forerunner of an inclination to travel in later life. From the simple and rational motives of travel and the sublimated needs of the spirit, to the compulsive unconscious impulses that can intensify into an obsession, traveling has many moods and many reasons.

Unconscious motives play an especially large role, for example, in the case of people whose ability to love is limited by certain conditions that can be fulfilled only through traveling. I once treated a man who had a very individual reason for his compulsive need to travel. He couldn't spend two nights in a row in the same city, in the same bed, and had to travel from place to place to the point of utter exhaustion. I saw him several times in my office and learned that this aversion to spending more than one night in the same bed in fact pertained not to the place or to the bed, but to a woman. To him, staying with a woman longer than one night meant making her into his mother, and thus sexually taboo. This is obviously a special case, but I believe that for many people traveling can have deep psychological meaning.

Of my later travels, Israel has perhaps left the strongest impressions on me. There I first became familiar with the Bible through direct experience. Our travels took us from David's grave in Jerusalem to the pillars of salt in Sodom on the Dead Sea, where the story of Lot is a reminder to women to control their proverbial curiosity. I must confess that the biblical remains moved me more than do the great sociological and industrial achievements of contemporary Israel.

I believe that my notes on Israel are objective, for both my past history and the detachment natural to my advanced age have made me a world citizen, and the ideals of my revolutionary youth in Poland have remained with me. My love for Israel is rooted chiefly in my loyalty to my husband, who stayed true to the cause of Zionism from his student years to the end of his life.

In his university days Felix became a devoted member of a Jewish student fraternity (*Kadimah*), which had been founded by Theodor Herzl to enable Jews to engage in dueling competitions with members of the national German dueling clubs. It was hard for those who knew Felix to believe that he belonged to a dueling fraternity. But his identification with the Jewish students who were assaulted by the bullying, arrogant German fraternity men in the corridors of the University of Vienna, was decisive. Among the German students themselves, an individual who had been personally insulted could gain satisfaction by challenging his antagonist to a formal duel. Until the formation of Kadimah, this right was not extended to Jews. Felix's indignation over these incidents made him a fighter (one such duel resulted in a serious eye injury that never completely healed).

His interest in Israel was responsible for our repeated visits to that country. Eventually he became involved in a special project: to study the paintings of Jewish children in Israel who had been driven out of their various countries by the Nazis. He found that in this way he could get to know their individual psychologies. This work was interrupted by his death; others have taken over his task, but, I discovered to my sorrow, they have not continued it in Felix's spirit.

As the story of my childhood indicates, I always identified myself intensely with Poland. Felix and I had stereotyped discussions on the subject, which never solved the disagreement between us: he regarded my nationality as Jewish; I, as Polish. But this never caused a real problem between us, for although Felix was an active Zionist, our sociopolitical ideals were not in conflict. Above all, we were in accord in our conception of man and his spiritual needs. Felix's death brought me closer to his Jewish ideology, for this had been a part of him, and it still is.

He made frequent visits to Israel; his work demanded them. I went with him to enjoy the incredible beauty of this country and to bring the Bible, which I hardly knew before visiting Israel, to life for myself in this way. During these visits, when, in contrast to my husband, I was practically undisturbed by lectures or social activities, I was free to wander at my leisure and without Baedeker, and so to come in contact with various kinds of people. On one visit we had with us a dear friend, Marianne Kris, whom I called "film-obsessed" because she lived in an unbroken state of symbiosis with her camera and took films of everything Israel had to offer, both animate and inanimate. I'll never forget the comic but pathetic scene that ensued when she once spotted through a window a class session in one of the orthodox schools in which the rabbi teaches young boys the Torah by repeating a passage over and over in a monotonous singsong. Suddenly becoming aware of their uninvited visitors, teacher and students rose together from their seats and ran wildly from the room, their *Bekesches* fluttering in the air and creating the impression of big black birds being chased away by a hunter!

I have a more antiquated method than Marianne Kris of preserving the sights I see on my travels. I never take photographs. I merely look about me, absorb fully the surroundings, and later I need only press a button of my memory apparatus in order to bring back images of the experiences I once lived so intensely.

As I write, the memories are returning to me by a kind of free association; in them our grandsons are gradually taking over our world into their control, as they have done in reality. With their appearance, the destinations of their grandparents' travels changed. Naturally we now went wherever we could visit them. Their father's scientific interests took the family to various European cultural centers. One of my son's sabbaticals, for instance, was spent in Rome, another in Paris. Felix and I eagerly waited for the signal, trying to organize our professional duties so as to be able to leave them behind. Soon we would be playing in the children's playground in the Bois de Boulogne, sailing in a swan-boat, and eating hot dogs ($1.50 for two) in an elegant restaurant on the Champs-Elysées. Another time we stood in the evening on a hill overlooking the Roman Forum, looking forward to the enchanting days ahead of us. We were not newcomers to Rome, but *this* visit was unique: it reunited us with our grandchildren, and carried a special joy. Yet when I look over Felix's bibliography and mine from those years, and reports of psychoanalytic meetings held then, it becomes clear to me that our devotion to our professional work never suffered from the intensity of our love for our grandsons.

My numerous visits to Rome had begun while I was still living in Vienna and continued throughout my stay in America. I must add that they were independent of Freud's love of this immortal city and not an expression of my identification with him.[1] My first visits were meant to be stops made in the course of Italian journeys, but none of Italy's other beauties excited my fantasy as much as Rome. So it often happened that though I came to the Eternal City with maps and an itinerary that was to take me farther south through Italy, I ignored these, preferring to spend my days exploring Rome. Every new trip to Rome awakened in me the feeling that I still didn't really know this city.

My last trip, in 1961, was a visit to my son and his family. He was spending that year on a Guggenheim Fellowship at a scientific institute in Frascati, doing experiments with a type of nuclear accelerator America didn't have as yet. He and his wife and children had a big house on the other side of the Tiber, in Trastevere; on its large flat roof I spent some of the most beauti-

1. *Vide* Freud's letters from Rome to his family.

ful hours of my life, for I had with me the people I loved best, and for the first time I could enjoy Rome as a resident instead of a tourist. I could submerge myself in the beauties of the Vatican in peace, at an hour when the crowds of tourists were still sleeping and the eternal places were not besieged by them.

By coincidence the rooms provided for us were in the Hotel Eden, where Freud had also lived at one time. I asked the hotel manager why he hadn't put up a plaque to commemorate the fact that Freud had lived there. He looked at me, his eyes blinking in surprise, and asked, "Who is Freud?"

I had previously seen Etruscan art in the Villa Giulia, and now that I had the time I eagerly set out to see more of it. My journey led me through Tarquinia, a medieval Italian city fascinating enough in itself. Here enthusiasm and impatience led me to climb down into the underground caves on whose stone walls Etruscan art has been forever preserved. The murals describe the daily lives of these people, who still offer riddles for scholars to solve.

Like every visitor to Rome, I left the ancient city with the feeling that once again I had managed to see only a tiny part of it. And as with most situations in life, this last trip also had its shadow: the tears of my beloved grandson Peter, about to be sent back to his school in French-speaking Switzerland, where he was unhappy. This parting saddened me very much. Some years later Peter returned to Rome to carry out a research project as a computer expert. And so Rome spread its glory into a third generation of Deutsches.

My travels in other parts of Italy—which, in effect, were bringing me to and from Rome—are harder to reanimate. But there is also an Italy that is not identical with Rome. There are little towns that offer their treasures especially to the traveler who crosses this marvelous country with his knapsack on his back, as I did once with two close women friends.

Venice enchanted us. For us it was not merely the city of the Piazza San Marco with its annoying pigeons, the Ponte dei

Sospiri, and the Grand Canal with its all too romantic gondoliers. Its fabulous treasures of art kept us there much longer than we had planned.

Here I must relate a small experience that sounds like a fairy tale: I was sitting with a friend at sunset in the famous café on the Piazza San Marco, and was just in the act of telling her that I had once been there many years ago (before 1910) with my friend L. At that very moment we saw him appear around the corner, like a *fata morgana*. Our joy was mingled with sadness, and all three of us tried to banish the strange aura of this encounter by talking animatedly about the loveliness of the churches of Venice.

Whenever I was free of the responsibilities of family and profession, I traveled without a planned itinerary, according to my moods and fantasies. Of all these excursions I remember the one to Siena especially well. My friend and I arrived at twilight at the hotel that had been recommended to us. Its windows looked out over the large *piazza*. Some young Italian students noticed us and promptly arranged a serenade under our windows. However, they were not rewarded with our personal thanks, as we were too tired, and perhaps also too mature, to enter into their youthful high spirits.

Now the sequence of events grows confused, and I see myself on a boat sailing into Naples harbor as the sun goes down, and I try to make sense of the expression, "See Naples and die." (As we later discovered, this expression has nothing to do with the city itself.) Dirt, and the desperate poverty, Pompeii with its impressive silence and its cabinet of secrets, and Vesuvius with its walks and, with luck, its tumultuous orange lava flows—these images remain. From Naples we went to Corsica, which had not yet been overrun by tourists. I could sit in the village square in Ajaccio and, completely unnoticed, watch the children playing and listen to the people conversing in what seemed to me some kind of Greek dialect.

Within the framework of my memoirs, the intellectual preparation for these trips and the cultural enrichment stemming from them are not worth going into. The literature on Italy is of course voluminous. In my early youth I was familiar with the writing of the famous Polish art historian Chłedowski, who has made huge contributions to the field. Bernard Berenson's book on the Italian Renaissance remained for me the most reliable guide in my travels through Italy despite modern scholars' doubts about its infallibility. In recent years the prominent English art historian Kenneth Clark, author of *Civilization*, has had an immense educational influence thanks to a method of presentation peculiarly suited to television. But this cannot replace the direct experience of an observant traveler.

Our visit to Spain turned out to be the most significant journey of my life, and the richest in experiences. Our decision to go was the outcome of a long inner struggle between conflicting considerations: on the one hand, there was Felix's health, which had to be spared, and also our strong protest against Franco's reactionary regime; on the other, our shared longing to see the beauties of this "forbidden" country. Elements of this fascination, which had intensified with time, were: Don Quixote, the clown with whom we felt we had so much in common; the beautiful, seductive Carmen, with her charming musical personification in the dramatic opera of Bizet; and above all, the tantalizing reports we had read and heard of springtime in Spain.

The final push toward carrying out this project came from an unlikely source. On the centennial of Freud's birthday, May 6, 1956, a large number of his students gathered in London to mourn at his grave. For years, this date had been a special day for psychoanalysts. During Freud's lifetime we used to call it "Orchid Day" for many of us knew of his love for this flower; on this day his house would be transformed into a garden of orchids— tokens of the world's love and respect for one of its great men.

Felix and I took part in the centennial ceremonies with renewed sadness. At the airport the customs officer asked us whether we had come to commemorate Freud's centenary; he added that all England grieved for her distinguished citizen. A small group of Freud's friends and pupils met with Anna Freud at her family home in London and Ernst Kris gave a solemn eulogy, which was transmitted by radio all over the city. We remembered Freud's love and admiration for England, which had certainly been justified when London opened her doors to him in his exile. We felt again the timelessness of grief: it seemed as if our beloved teacher had died only yesterday. (Personally, I still have not accepted his death; often I have the feeling that I have just spoken with him or, as if I were in a state of delusion, am planning to visit him.)

Felix and I had no desire to return to our professional activities; these were so closely bound up with Freud! We wanted to escape from them into some new experience. Spain seemed to be the right destination for us.

Our trip began with an excursion to the island of Majorca. At the time I was very busy with my study of George Sand, and I wished to see the spots where she and many other writers had found inspiration, and where Chopin had written his sentimental, romantic compositions. I hear that by now the island has been completely profaned by hotels, restaurants, and sensation-seeking tourists, but when we visited Majorca it was still comparatively unspoiled. We spent some pleasant days there before continuing on our way.

The formalities of this journey have faded, but our experience of Spain has remained sharp and clear: the fragrant and colorful springtime, the monasteries and their monks, the charming architecture of the houses, the art, bullfights, palaces, museums, aristocratic *señoritas*, vulgar gypsies, snow-covered peaks of the Pyrenees. All these stored impressions now whirl at a quick tempo across the screen of my memory.

How differently each of us, Felix and I, experienced the beauty of the journey! I was overwhelmed by emotion and tried to control it through the intellectual objectivity of an observer. I read travel books and tried to find the places described in them. Felix too tried to keep his upsurges of emotion under control by expressing them through art. He continually jotted down notes and made sketches, and when we came back to the hotel room in the evenings he would usually sit down in some dim corner and draw for me what we had seen that day. These were typical moments in which his love and desire to share with me awakened the talents he would otherwise have allowed to lie unused. What has become of those little drawings of Spain, which we left behind us somewhere in our wanderings?

In Seville, when I asked for Carmen at the old cigar factory at the city gate, a crowd of toothless working women came out. Many of them were named Carmen, but when they finally understood which Carmen I was looking for, they declared to me in chorus, *"Esta e morta."* But nobody in Seville said to me that Don Quixote was dead, for he still lives in the hearts of Spain's youth in the full force of his fantasy existence. Besides, a thorough knowledge of *Don Quixote* is obligatory in Spanish high schools!

We were very happy together in Spain. It was our first journey since the birth of our grandsons that did not lead to *them!* Spain was for us alone. Never in our then forty-four-year-old marriage had we been so free from pressures, so free to enjoy ourselves, as we were on this visit to Spain. We felt a sensation of uniqueness that was entirely subjective, for our itinerary merely retraced the much-traveled paths taken by all tourists in Spain.

I burned with eagerness to be in Granada, and I was glad to find out when we arrived that the fountains were not working, because the water system needed repairs. I thought to myself: now I can wander around and listen to the stories told by the harem walls, which have witnessed so much. Perhaps I was waiting to hear about scenes of wild spitefulness and jealousy among the wives of the respectably polygamous men of the past. . . . No, not a word of hate came from the whispering walls, only tales of glowing homosexual love in which the husband and the eunuchs were the only disturbance. A Turkish woman lawyer who has made a study of jurisprudence and its bearing on sexual relationships in Turkey and its neighboring countries, told me that whenever monogamy was legally instituted in a Moslem land there was an epidemic of suicides among the women: the new laws deprived them of the possibility of gratifying their homosexual love. Such liaisons were frequent in the harems.

Let me now turn to my impressions of the Spanish men—the *señores* whose dancing silhouettes, with slender bodies and protruding buttocks, are well known to us from flamenco dances. To the traveler, the image of the Spanish toreador may be a symbol of virility; if so, this is of course only a subjective impression created by a prearranged situation.

Bullfighting, Spain's national sport, is a rigidly formalized ritual in which men and animals fight to the death: thus the aggressive drives of the spectators, both men and women, all ecstatically carried away by the performance, are vicariously satisfied. The involvement of the spectators was more upsetting to me than the fight itself: it was an orgy of released aggressions. The young bull that was led into the arena made the greatest impression on me as a sober observer: "Ferdinand the Bull," as I called this anonymous animal, seemed to me the most *human* creature in the whole crowded expanse of the arena. I've heard that the culmination of the aggressions thus mobilized comes after the fight, when the Spanish masses enjoy with orgiastic pleasure the meat of the conquered bull, prepared with more or less culinary skill.

Of course it is difficult for a psychoanalyst to remain satisfied with the general statement that the bullfight is a release and a gratification of aggression. I consider this merely a banal truth, and I realize that the whole psychological situation is much more complicated, as the long ceremonies and rigid rules seem to indicate.

In retelling my unforgettable experiences in Spain, I cannot leave out the journey from Madrid to Seville, which we made partly by car and partly on foot. Thus we had the good fortune not only to see the blossom-filled spring and the small houses of the provincial towns with their enchanting courtyards, but also to speak with the inhabitants of the provinces in our broken Spanish.

Unfortunately, everywhere we went we saw, with suppressed rage, Franco's spies joining the tourists in order to entice them into viewing Franco's "accomplishments on behalf of social progress." Their trump card was the hospitals, in which the workers did indeed receive the best of care, bordering on luxury; however, these hospital tours are supposed to make the observer forget that the fundamental rights to organize into labor unions and to go on strike, achieved decades ago by other European workers, remain forbidden in Spain.

Our visit ended with a long look at Gibraltar and Algeciras, where we promised ourselves to make our planned trip to Africa a reality as soon as possible. But destiny had willed otherwise. . . .

My next trip to Europe was to Greece, *à trois* with Lucie Jessner and Eleanor Pavenstedt, who took over for her two passive friends the burdens of reality: hotel arrangements, etc. It is hard for me to describe the enchantment of this journey, even though I have kept every step of it so intensively in my memory that I sometimes think I could easily take over the role of a guide. Here as nowhere else the visual part of my memory still serves me perfectly. For many people, the pace of this trip would have been exhausting, because it led us to all parts of Greece: the "classical" part, which included Schliemann's archaeological excavations, as well as the Aegean islands, including Crete. We had a wonderful guide whose ambition was to show us everything in Greece that had not been taken away by Albion's eager hands.

There was one thing that sometimes hurt my conscience: my husband did not accompany me on this trip. At this time his health had started to decline, and he had the feeling that he did not have much time left to finish his work. It was only his insistence that I go to Greece which overpowered my feeling of painful anxiety for him. Also, I think I felt darkly that this might be the last time that I could enjoy the beauty of life still free from grief. It is clear that he was making an effort not to interfere with my plans to see the country I had longed to visit since my early youth. At various stations of our trip there were cards from Felix indicating how well his work was going and how much his health was improving. Mutual friends confirmed his bulletins; but soon after my return he collapsed without recovering, and this was the beginning of the end.

Whenever remorse invades my peace of mind, I remind myself that my compassion and complete dedication to him in the last months of his life may have been my expiation. Greece became an unreachable magic land closed to me forever. Only some years after Felix's death did I allow myself through my work on Dionysus and Apollo (directly inspired by that trip) to revive in my mind places that had become in a measure taboo. From time to time Lucie sends me books reminding me of Greece. It is again the wisdom of her heart that is speaking. Sometimes Lucie indicates in her delicate way her readiness to repeat the experience, but feels my definite "no" and understands the cause.

After Felix's death in 1964 I had to go through a very painful period of mourning. I thought that I would never again be able to have a positive outlook towards life. All who had known him, especially the children in our family, were overwhelmed by deep mourning. I loved these children too much to allow myself the luxury of unrestrained grief.

I began to search for some work that would at least occupy my mind during this difficult time. It would have been impossible for me to work on Felix's biography just then. It was also quite clear to all of us that this labor ought to be undertaken by someone more objective than I. A committee designated by the Psychoanalytic Society elected Dr. Sanford Gifford, a great admirer of Felix and thoroughly familiar with his work, to write a biography with special emphasis on Felix's scientific findings. This book seems to be approaching completion. I consider Sanford the most outstanding scientific mind of the younger generation of analysts. His wife Ingrid, also a therapist, often hides her great knowledge of medicine and her skill in therapeutic work with patients behind her household activities, yet I regard her professional capacities very highly and so do other analysts. My personal friendship with the Giffords is a very important element in my now-lonely life. They remain my chief source of information on current events in the Boston Psychoanalytic Society, in which I am now a stranger with a "brilliant" past!

At any rate, the writing of Felix's biography was being taken care of. What was left for me to do? Instead of treating individual patients, I began to write a book about adolescents, with emphasis on group formation. I had always had an interest in adolescence, and it was not difficult for me, despite my mourning, to work with adolescents and to write about them. A stream of teenagers started coming to my house regularly, enticed by their friends' reports that there was a strange woman in Cambridge to whom you could go and talk about anything you pleased. The group of forty-four adolescents whom I interviewed periodically over the next two years of course included a number of girls, and perhaps it was my identification with them that opened the way to an autobiographical description of my own adolescence.

Since my husband's death I have withdrawn almost completely from my work at the Boston Psychoanalytic Institute (my active collaboration ended when my husband and I both reached the mandatory retirement age of seventy). I rarely attend the meetings and generally keep away from the social life of its members. I respect the young generation—they know more about new developments, organizations, etc., than I do. They study analysis and read Freud's works, generally as preparation for seminars, discussions, etc. But I don't necessarily find in all of them a deep emotional experience of psychoanalysis and of Freud's genius. The difference between my own enthusiasm for Freud and these young people's reaction to him as "required reading" reminds me of how in my youth I was shaken by emotion as I read the *Iliad* and the *Odyssey,* whereas students at the "classical" high school in Vienna, where Homer was part of the regular curriculum, thought of these works with boredom and dread.

But I also know some of those who read Freud without being required to do so; they are close to me personally. Others know Freud almost by heart. They discuss endlessly what Freud meant by this or that expression, and are in the process of making psychoanalysis into a kind of Talmudic discipline.

I regret the great dependence of future analysts on control analyses, for I find that the best way to learn is through independent experience. The control analyst should exercise his advisory role only in difficult situations. I believe that I am justified in making this criticism because of my long-standing interest in the problems of control analysis and my contributions to their solution (see p. 163). This overdependence on controls makes psychoanalysis into something it is not and should not be: a method that can be learned like any other scientific discipline. The candidates expect to have this only partially learnable process made fully learnable: still another supervisor, and another! When I was a training analyst I regarded the controls largely as a protection for the patients—beyond this, I think that in every learning process one gains most from the mistakes one makes. Besides, here as in all analytic procedures, each analyst has his personal touch. The young analyst should not overburden his individuality with too many "required" influences. Problems inevitably arise. But I deplore greatly the fact that supervision can become a mania for some, and lead to an evasion of responsibility and independence. This has been my experience with many candidates encountered over the years. Sometimes I have the feeling that analysis in general now includes too much organization and obligatory teaching and learning. More and more, I feel like someone who has been working in an artist's studio and suddenly finds himself in a factory.

I have heard that I am beginning to become a kind of myth to some. However, I hope that this autobiography will remind the younger generation that I still have an earthly body and that I participate emotionally in their achievements in the service of psychoanalysis. Despite my retirement, the bonds I have formed during the years of my work in psychoanalysis have not been broken. On Christmas and my birthday every year the house is filled with flowers sent by pupils and colleagues. My contact with the younger generation continues, and I often have the opportunity to communicate fruitfully the experiences of my long life dedicated to psychoanalysis.

Looking over the list of my pupils, I notice that the majority of them have been men. Some of them have become scientific and professional leaders, Robert Wälder and Ernst Kris for example. Altogether I have had four kinds of pupils, binding Vienna and the United States together: first the Viennese; next the Americans who came to be trained in Vienna; and later, Americans in their homeland and those European refugees who, like me, went through the process of Americanization but conserved the tradition of Freud's personal influence.

I am sometimes astonished that nowadays there are so few women in psychoanalytic training, because I believe that psychoanalysis is *par excellence* a profession for women. One thing that I do not like about the women who are currently studying for this profession is that, according to my information, many of them are timing their pregnancies to fit the schedule of their psychoanalytic training. I would prefer to see a more spontaneous approach to motherhood.

In the ever-threatening vast loneliness of old age, personal friendships become islands of refuge. When younger friends are successful in their work, the blows to one's narcissism are made less traumatic through identification with them. A small group of intimate friends, old and young, helps me to cope with the inevitable deprivations of my existence. My children and grandchildren, including my daughter-in-law Suzanne, fill with devotion an old woman's increasing needs for loving care. The blessing of my own capacity to love and to be deeply interested in others is still with me.

My old relationships with people have created a kind of insurance against loneliness. I have already spoken about the surviving members of the Black Cat; some of their children have carried on their parents' friendships as a sort of inheritance. With some of my younger friends, I have the feeling that the difference in our ages is shrinking with time. Those who were once "too young" for me have annihilated the barriers of age by their personal qualities. For example, Ruth and Kurt Eissler became in America not only my friends but also occasionally my advisers on scientific and professional matters. I must say that nothing has increased my analytic understanding of Goethe and Shakespeare as much as Kurt's writings. His latest book, *Talent and Genius,* fulfills with great erudition the need for a new biographical approach to Freud's genius.[1]

Ralph M. Kaufman and Dorian Feigenbaum became prominent on the list of those who compensated Felix and me for friendships lost to us through the cruelties of life. Ralph—or Mo, as he is usually called—was the first to welcome my husband to America and introduce him to Beth Israel Hospital in Boston, just before Felix's association with Dr. Stanley Cobb. Sadly for me, he moved from Boston to New York to become the head of the psychiatric department at Mount Sinai Hospital, but this separation never weakened our friendship. When the Boston Psychoanalytic Institute honored Felix and me with the establishment of the Felix and Helene Deutsch Prize, Ralph Kaufman and Ernst Kris read papers commemorating the occasion. I always hoped that Mo Kaufman's retirement from Mount Sinai Hospital would bring him back as a full-time analyst to Boston, but Israel won him—he became a teacher of analysis in that country. Dorian Feigenbaum, one of the founders of the *Psychoanalytic Quarterly,* remained a devoted friend until the end of

1. *Talent and Genius: The Fictitious Case of Tausk Contra Freud* (Chicago: Quadrangle Books, 1971).

his short life. This friendship was succeeded after his untimely death by one with his brother, Aryeh Feigenbaum, who until his retirement was head of the department of ophthalmology of the University of Jerusalem Hospital and author of a number of interesting publications, especially on the psychology of languages.

As I've mentioned, although my active affiliation with the Psychoanalytic Society has become more and more restricted, my interest in its activities is still very vivid. Today its membership numbers 120, and there are a great many working committees. Besides the regular teaching organization, the Society has created an important new office, now filled by Dr. James Mann: that of dean, to act as a liaison figure between the various committees. A number of the Society's younger members still turn to me, the old veteran, for advice; fortunately my psychoanalytic memory is still stubbornly resisting the deterioration due to old age. In recent years it has sometimes happened that a younger, or more often a middle-aged, analyst will greet me with the words. "I had my first control case with you." Sometimes they are amazed when I remember the case in greater detail than they do. I know why this is: generally I've grasped the architectonic structure of the case, and the image of its psychic architecture allows me to keep in my memory the basic form and also the individual features of the case.

I do not miss my previous activity and I am contented with the progress being made by the third generation of analysts, whose parents were my pupils, or even members of the the Black Cat. Many of them have become the avant-garde of psychoanalysis, as their parents were before them.

I remember one of my conversations with Freud on the future of psychoanalysis. In this talk Freud touched upon the idea of the "splendid isolation" of analysis and said prophetically that one day psychoanalysis would be taught as a regular course of study in the universities. I was not in favor of this, and I regret that his prophecy has to a large extent come true.

There was a time when I felt responsible, so to speak, for everything that happened in the field of analysis. But now I have given up this narcissistic identification, and I am resolved to entrust the future to younger analysts. Many of them are attempting to subordinate analysis to social developments and to hold society responsible for psychological phenomena. Freud himself says about this relationship:

The fateful question of the human species seems to me to be whether and to what extent the cultural process developed in it will succeed in mastering the derangements of communal life caused by the human instincts of aggression and self-destruction. In this connection, perhaps the phase through which we are at this moment passing deserves special interest. Men have brought their powers of subduing the forces of nature to such a pitch that by using them they could now very easily exterminate one another to the last man. They know this—hence arises a great part of their current unrest, their dejection, their mood of apprehension. And now it may be expected that the other of the two "heavenly forces", eternal Eros, will put forth his strength so as to maintain himself alongside of his equally immortal adversary.[1]

1. *Civilization and Its Discontents,* trans. James Strachey (New York: W.W. Norton & Company, 1962), p. 92.

XIV

In Retrospect

I N W R I T I N G this autobiography it has been easier for me to speak about the past than the present, for the patina of time has enhanced and mellowed my own experiences, softened my sense of blame towards others, and made me more tolerant of my own shortcomings.

I have tried to stay within the narrow framework of an autobiography and to speak only of the events relevant to my own life—even when these events in themselves seemed to reach far beyond the scope of my individual history. In the course of this writing, the difficulties of maintaining the proper degree of objectivity have sometimes seemed insurmountable, especially when the events described are not merely history but refer to the present. It has been easier for me to write about Grandfather Leizor and his mean hypocrisy than about my beloved and admired father, and easier to write about my father than about Felix and my children, especially my grandsons, whose joys and sorrows are a vivid part of my own emotional life.

While working on this manuscript I have noticed that often

apparently irrelevant memories have intruded into my train of thought, making it impossible for me to follow a logically controlled path. Such intrusions are usual and expected events in psychoanalysis, but any situation in which the usual controls of the consciousness are relaxed may lead to them.

For help in describing events of my life, I have turned to my previous writings. In Volume II of *The Psychology of Women* I described my own pregnancy and the birth of my son in an impersonal, generalized form. When I began writing my autobiography, these chapters came like a *deus ex machina* to my aid; my description of the biological and psychological processes of pregnancy could be borrowed back again from this old book.

I am glad that my younger colleagues have been able to confirm through their own observations the conclusions I drew from my direct experience in *The Psychology of Women*. Many girls and women have told me of the psychological accuracy of this work, even in recent times, when social developments have in many respects made it outdated.

I have tried to invest this autobiography with a character that is very personal and at the same time objectively impersonal. The general psychological and biological observations have been much easier to communicate than my personal experiences. But I have tried to do justice to both aspects of my writing.

As I look back over my life, I can discern recurrent patterns that knit together my childhood, maturity, and old age. The emotional patterns of later years are a continuation of childhood patterns, and this fact can easily be illustrated from my own experiences. The childhood anxiety that something dreadful would happen to my father on his way back from the nightly card game at his club (p. 40) reappeared from time to time in my relationship to my son, and again even more intensely in connection with my older grandson Peter. My son's house in Cambridge is not far from ours; when Peter was born, a room on the ground floor became his nursery. Every night I would take a walk past my children's house to see for myself whether there was a light on in my newborn grandson's room. I was filled with totally irrational fears that Peter might be kidnapped.

Interestingly, both of these fears, for my father and for Peter, were associated with windows: I am either outside a window trying to see what is going on in the room, or I am inside trying to see what is going on in the street. As a psychoanalyst I understood my own "repetition tendency" and recognized the emotional pattern of the Oedipal situation of my childhood. In both anxiety situations, I fear that somebody I dearly love is in grave danger and that I am unable to save him. In both situations I am physically separated from the object of my anxieties and cannot communicate with him directly. In both cases someone else has the role of protector—my beloved "belongs" to another woman. In the case of my father it was my mother who had the best right to worry about him. Now it was my daughter-in-law who had priority in the loving care of the little boy. I did not feel hostility toward her as my apparent competitor; I was merely irrationally afraid that she would somehow not be careful enough to prevent Peter from being kidnapped. At the moment of this writing I feel that we can both relinquish our vigilance for Peter to my beloved granddaughter-in-law, Barbara.

It would take me too far away from the stream of my reportage if I were to mention and analyze all the occasions on which lighted windows mobilized my anxiety and frustrations.

The strongest emotional experience of my recent life has been the loss of my husband and my never-ending grief. My love for Felix lives on in my love for my children and grandchildren. My capacity for giving love seems to me to be unchanged. As for receiving love . . . I feel loved in spite of the fact that old people are seldom loved; they bear too much of *memento mori.* By now I have outlived most of the people I loved in the past. During the writing of these memoirs I revived many ghosts of the past, only to find that in reality they had never left me—they have become part of me.

The biological destiny of old age varies from one individual to another. Like all the developmental periods of life, it depends greatly on the events of adolescence. To our stereotyped way of thinking, the process of growing up is identical with the conquest of the stormy forces of adolescence. Yet I feel that my *Sturm und Drang* period, which continued long into my years of maturity, is still alive within me and refuses to come to an end. This feeling is supported by the continuation of relationships that span three generations. I find that there are still ecstasies and loves in me, and that these feelings are rooted in my adolescence. They may be reaction formations against the threat of death, but at the same time they represent the generous impulses of the most energetic period of my life.

This happy circumstance has sometimes brought me into situations that clash with the evidence of old age. For example, some years ago I marched in an anti-war demonstration at the invitation of my colleagues and pupils. I was attired in my white doctor's coat, as were the other doctors marching with me. I was the only old person there, and I felt embarrassed—until I discovered that the reaction of my young colleagues was enthusiastic. Appearently I was the only one who had fears that my action was anarchronistic.

All the best human impulses can be traced back to adolescence. I believe that these persistent adolescent forces are the best aspect of my own old age. Looking back over my description of my adolescence in this writing, we can retrace their development and see old age not as an inversion but as a harmonious consequence.

My scientific and ideological identity remains with Freud and with most of my old friendships that still remain. My intellectual powers of course now function under the limits placed on them by old age, but are still capable of independent work. The question of my creativity finds a partial answer in the writing of this autobiography.

The ideas of Freud always had for me the character of a categorical imperative. I was aware that I had a mission in

America given to me by him: "I . . . hope, with you, that you will accomplish as much good [in America] as you have here." I have done my best. I have worked within the framework of psychoanalysis as a science and a method of treatment. I have participated in the achievements and the controversies of the psychoanalytic movement here. I have written numerous psychoanalytic papers and several books. But at the close of this epilogue, I confess for the first time even to myself that despite my complete and unchanged dedication to Freud and his teaching, after more than fifty years of uninterrupted activity in the service of psychoanalysis I now wish for nothing more than a very long sabbatical.